CW00691386

The Scott Gallery: A Series Of One Hundred And Forty-six Photogravures, Together With Descriptive Letterpress, Volume 1...

Sir James Lewis Caw

SCOTTISH PORTRAITS

SCOTTISH PORTRAITS

WITH AN HISTORICAL AND CRITICAL
INTRODUCTION AND NOTES BY
JAMES L. CAW
CURATOR, SCOTTISH NATIONAL PORTRAIT GALLERY

VOLUME I

NEMO ME IMPVNE LACESSIT

EDINBURGH : T. C. & E. C. JACK
AND 34 HENRIETTA STREET, LONDON, W.C.
1903

Edinburgh: T. and A. Constable, Printers to His Majesty

CONTENTS

v

SCOTTISH PORTRAITS

CONTENTS

THE editor and publishers desire to express
their great indebtedness to the private owners
and the keepers of public collections who
have allowed portraits in their possession or
care to be reproduced. Without such co-
operation a really representative series of
historical portraits would be impossible; and
in the case of 'Scottish Portraits' it was so
cordial that permission was received at once
for all but two of the hundred and twenty
portraits originally chosen, and of the persons
represented in these, other pictures, equally
interesting, were readily obtained.

INTRODUCTION

INTRODUCTION

THE spirit of romance is strong in Scottish history. From the time when, on the very verge of its written records, the Roman legions failed to subdue the ancient Celtic peoples until to-day, the quality of fascination is rarely absent from the story of the Scottish nation, for by temperament, or through stress of circumstances, the Scots seem to possess the faculty of doing things in that picturesque fashion which appeals to the imagination and the heart. And this romantic history has often been individualised, as it were, in a most striking way in the persons of the chief actors in its great events. Individuality is indeed characteristic of the race, and in no country is the memory of its illustrious dead more revered. Carlyle's complaint that the German galleries contain 'no likeness at all, or next to none at all, of the noble Human Realities, or of any part of them, who have sprung, not from the idle brains of dreaming *dilettanti*, but from the head of God Almighty to make this poor authentic earth a little memorable for us, and to do a little work that may be eternal there,' cannot be applied to Scotland, for Scottish painters have excelled in portraiture, and in the Scottish galleries are to be found, not a complete collection indeed, but many portraits of the great ones of the past. Yet these offer but an inadequate survey of the field. The spirit, which makes the nation proud of her past, extends to the more intimate relationship of the family, and in consequence most of the finest portraits remain in private hands. It was therefore only by drawing principally on these sources that such a series as the present was possible.

During the Middle Ages, the condition of the country was, socially and politically, too tumultuous, and, financially, too poor to permit the practice on a considerable scale of any art save architecture for defence in this world or for preparation for the next. That there were beautiful things, ecclesiastical and domestic furniture, embroideries, enamels, tapestries, and such like, in Scotland, old records and relics prove; but many of them were of foreign origin, and there was little room in an ill-lit Scottish keep or in a flat in Edinburgh or Stirling High Street for art collections, even though there had been money to buy them. Of pictorial art the traces are still scantier. Even of portraiture, which is the branch most likely to leave prized records, for other than artistic reasons will tend to preserve them, there are few existing examples. Of the heroes of the great and unequal but successful struggle with a powerful neighbour for national existence there is no record, pictured or sculptured; of the brave but rude and lawless barons, who were for ever contesting the authority of the Crown, there is no trace, except here and there a mutilated and unrecognisable effigy; the monuments of the great churchmen have been rifled and ruined; of the poets who joined in wordy flightings at the court of the Stuart kings there was probably never a likeness made. From before the Reformation, during the course of which much art-work was destroyed or taken out of the country, scarce a dozen authentic portraits remain. That there were many more is probable, for if there were few artists resident in or visiting Scotland, and none of note (those mentioned in the Treasurer's accounts are untraceable), the mediæval Scot, like his present-day descendant, was often a great wanderer, and, following the fashion of countries in which he chanced to sojourn, would have his portrait painted. But the suggestion may be hazarded that pictorial art had little hold in Scotland, and, in any case, the earliest Scottish portraits that survive are invariably of foreign workmanship.

Portraiture in Scotland opens with a masterpiece of Flemish painting. Although critical opinion at present tends to crystallise in the attribution to Van der Goes (died 1482), of whose art only one perfectly authenticated example remains, the authorship of the Trinity College altarpiece is not yet settled. All that is certain is that it is one of the finest works of its school and time, and that it contains portraits of James III. and his queen, Margaret of Denmark, and of Sir Edward Boncle, provost of the church from which it takes its name. And other portraits of this and slightly later date, such as those of Bishop Elphinstone at Aberdeen University and Carberry Tower; of Margaret Tudor, Queen of James IV.; of James V., and of his daughter Queen Mary and her supporters or antagonists, are usually either of Flemish or French origin, in the earlier part of the sixteenth century usually the first, in the later frequently the second. For the most part also, it is impossible to assign the pictures to their respective painters. Here and there, as in the case of the Margaret Tudor in the Scottish National Portrait Gallery, there is little doubt whose hand has been at work; a few likenesses of Mary Stuart can be given almost certainly to a particular painter; and some pictures of the great nobles are

INTRODUCTION

either signed by the artist or otherwise attested; but in the majority of cases one has to be content with unknown painter of a known school.

Even more puzzling than the game of attribution is the difficulty of determining what opportunities certain people could have of being painted in the way they were. It is scarcely possible, for instance, that an artist of the gifts shown in the Trinity College altarpiece could be in Scotland without leaving some other pictorial trace of his visit: it is quite impossible that James and his queen could have been painted from the life in Bruges or Ghent. And, to take another of the portraits already mentioned, careful comparison of the movements of painter and sitter makes it unlikely that Mabuse ever saw the heroine of Dunbar's most famous poem. One is forced, therefore, to conclude that many portraits of this period were painted from drawings or other authentic materials supplied to the painter. That this is probable is borne out by what is known of the conditions under which many artists then worked; by such proclamations as Elizabeth's forbidding any but approved painters to paint portraits of Her Majesty; and by the existence of collections of drawings like that gathered by the Duc d'Aumale at Chantilly, or the one at Arras which contains several drawings of fifteenth and sixteenth century Scots—Bernard Stuart, Sieur of Aubigny (1447?-1508), and Alexander Stuart, bastard of James IV. and Archbishop of St. Andrews (1493?-1513), to name two of the most interesting—and of the Sieur de la Bastie and other French adventurers in Scotland of whom painted portraits are unknown. In some other cases, and of this Holbein's practice is typical, pictures were painted from drawings from life by the artist himself. With well-authenticated portraits these building-up processes are of little account, of course; but in many cases there is less to go by, and one has to rest satisfied with the names traditionally attached. And where the portrait has a good and probable history, belongs to the period, and is not contradicted by contemporary written descriptions (often contradictory themselves), there is much to be said for tradition. To reject portraits such as that of the Regent Moray at Holyrood, because one cannot demonstrate conclusively that it represents him, is to carry scepticism farther than is desirable.

Previous to the beginning of the seventeenth century there are, as I have said, comparatively few Scottish portraits of which one can be absolutely certain as regards both subject and painter; but it is fortunate that we have as many reliable likenesses as there are. Amongst those reproduced here are portraits of eight or nine Stuart kings and queens, of two of the greatest churchmen of the old faith, and of the two Reformers who were most largely instrumental in its overthrow; the Lords of the Congregation are represented by Moray and Morton; the Hamilton faction by Arran; Queen Mary's cause by Lethington, Kirkcaldy of Grange, and the 'loyal' Seton; accomplishment and scholarship by the 'Admirable' Crichton, George Buchanan, and Napier of Merchiston. And to these as many more, with scarcely less call for reproduction, could have been added easily, if the claims of the following three hundred years could have been ignored. There is not, however, a single portrait amongst them that one could pronounce with any degree of certainty to be by a Scottish painter. Yet such there seems to have been. In the Treasurer's accounts there are numerous entries of payments to such and such a 'payntour,' perhaps a visitor but no less probably a native, and in 1579, when portraits of Knox and Buchanan were sent to Beza in Geneva to be engraved for his *Icones* (1580)—only the former appeared—the accompanying letter stated plainly that there were painters in Scotland. But it is significant that amongst the authentic portraits of Queen Mary there is not one that was painted at home. The joyous days of her youth in France and the sad years of her English imprisonment have their portraits; but, except the rude effigies on her coinage, nothing remains to show how she looked during her reign in her own country.

A number of Scottish portraits, unique in themselves or valuable as contemporary evidence with which to test painted portraits, are to be found also in books of the late sixteenth and the seventeenth centuries, some published at home, some abroad.

It was not until the beginning of the seventeenth century that a genuinely Scottish, and fully recognisable, painter emerged. George Jamesone of Aberdeen, often styled the Scottish Van Dyck, was born about the close of the sixteenth century. In 1612 he was apprenticed as 'paynter' to a kinsman in Edinburgh, but, having abandoned the trade for the profession of painting, he next appears as the author of a portrait of a Lord Provost of Aberdeen (1620). From then until his death in 1644 he produced many portraits of members of the great Scottish families, which remain amongst the most tangible records of that troubled time. Keeping aloof from politics, he was employed by both Royalists and Covenanters, and even his extant works form a very complete gallery of the distinguished people of his generation. Argyll, Montrose, Johnston of Warriston, Marischal, Southesk, Hope, Arthur Johnston—all these and many more figure on his canvases, and enable us to realise more vividly what manner of men and women

INTRODUCTION

moulded the destinies of Scotland in the momentous period which followed the
union of the Crowns. And as Jamesone was peculiarly free from artistic affectation, and was primarily interested in his sitters as persons, he, as a rule, represented
them in everyday dress. Armour seldom figures in his pictures: compared with
most of his contemporaries, he was a domestic portrait-painter. He is said to have
painted miniatures, but none can be identified as his; and of the many full-
lengths of large size attributed to him I have not seen one in which his hand is
traceable. His characteristic pieces are bust portraits, 'to the waist' as he put it
in a letter; and of the general type of his work those reproduced are representative.
To a great extent he must have been self-taught, for the tradition that sent him
to Antwerp to study with Van Dyck in Rubens's atelier has been exploded. Yet
the Flemish-like look of his work is undeniable, and the dignity and sobriety of
the refined and simple convention he somehow acquired, palliates his rather
archaic and mannered drawing, which, however, often suggests character very
fully. His pictures have a certain grave beauty of their own.

Jamesone's portraits form the greater part of the pictorial record of the Scots
of his day, but union with England led many of the greater nobles over the Border,
and the painters, whom James VI.'s and Charles I.'s encouragement brought to
London, have left many portraits of Scots men and women also. Van Somer
(1576-1621), Cornelius Janssen (1590-1665), Daniel Mytens (1590?-1642), Van
Dyck himself, contribute to the painted records of the first half of the seventeenth
century, as Lely (1617-1680), Kneller (1648-1723), and others do to that of its
closing years. And from Jamesone onward a certain number of Scottish painters
were always at work. Immediately after his death, indeed, all artistic effort seems
to have been smothered by the armed struggle between Covenant and King and
then between Covenanted King and Commonwealth, but shortly after the Restoration we find Michael Wright and the Scougalls and their pupils painting. Wright
(1625?-1700), who was by far the ablest of these native artists and a man of real
artistic gifts, as portraits like those of Sir William Bruce, the architect, and the
English philosopher, Hobbes, prove, went to England, however, and although
John Scougall (1645?-1730?) produced a number of good portraits, his average
was not high—his son and his pupils were considerably his inferiors—and about
1685 the Duke of Queensberry brought Nicolas Hude to Scotland to paint
portraits. Hude had no great success; but Sir John Medina (1659-1710), who
came on the guarantee of Lord Leven a few years later, was highly popular,
and is said to have filled the country with portraits in which, we are told, the

bodies, clad in armour or swathed in meaningless draperies, were painted beforehand and stocked, only the heads being added to order. Yet unequal and mannered as his work often is, at its best it has character, and is vigorously and boldly, if rather coarsely, painted. It gave satisfaction to his clients; he made money, and the Duke of Queensberry made him a knight, the last created before the union of 1707. To him we owe portraits of men like Dalrymple, Hamilton, and Seafield, and from him William Aikman, the most conspicuous Scottish painter of the early eighteenth century, received his first lessons.

A Forfarshire laird, Aikman (1682-1731) sold the ancestral acres to become a painter and went to Rome, where he studied for some years. On his return he settled in Edinburgh, but had difficulty in making a decent living, and in 1723, on the suggestion of John, Duke of Argyll, he decided to go to London. There he associated with the learned and cultured, and some of his most interesting portraits represent authors with whom he was friendly. His work is marked by refinement and grace rather than by power or passion, and his colour is apt to be grey and cold. Yet his best portraits reveal considerable power of characterisation and quiet dignity of style. Aikman had for contemporaries in Scotland a number of painters of little account, and it was not until the son of his friend Allan Ramsay, wig-maker and poet, had followed his example and studied in Italy, that he had a worthy successor in the Scottish capital. But Ramsay (1713-1784) also was lured south by the greater scope and fame of a London career. A man of considerable learning and literary talent, he mixed much in literary society and was the intimate of Johnson, Rousseau, and David Hume, of the two latter of whom he left admirable portraits. He had distinct gifts as a painter, and his finest work is accomplished technically, while his portraits, particularly of women, have frequently great charm. A *persona grata* at court, he was appointed—and Reynolds was alive—painter to King George III., a royal favour which ensured a large and lucrative connection. This great practice, and latterly his love for Italy, led to the employment of a regular staff of assistants who, during his long absences, carried on the business. More than anything else this accounts for the inequality and the formality of much of the work that came from his studio, and detracts from the position to which his finest things entitle him.

Amongst Ramsay's assistants were several who have contributed to the interest of Scottish portraiture. David Martin (1736-1798), who had been his master's favourite, and whose art, if less refined, partakes of a similar character, painted a goodly number of Scottish celebrities; and Alexander Nasmyth (1758-1840),

INTRODUCTION

before he turned his attention to landscape, and in so doing became 'the father of Scottish landscape,' produced many portraits, mostly of cabinet size, of which those of Burns are by far the most famous. Contemporary with these were others: Skirving (1749-1819), the pastelist, and Brown (1752-1787), the black-and-white draughtsman, who were purely portrait-painters; Alexander Runciman (1736-1785), who varied his ambitious but incomplete figure pieces with portraits; and David Allan (1744-1796), who turned from portraiture to make those illustrations to *The Gentle Shepherd*, and to Scottish song and story in which one finds the germ of Scottish *genre* painting. Except that they now and then painted some one of importance, Seton and Davison and others are of little account. But the Tassies, James (1735-1799) and William (1717-1860), must not be forgotten for their medallions, in a glassy paste of considerable beauty, are admirable in their kind, and form a most valuable contribution to the pictured history of the eighteenth century. Nor can the caricaturist, John Kay (1742-1880), be completely ignored. Innocent of art as his etchings are, they not infrequently express with vividness the more salient points of some prominent character.

This was the great period in English portrait-painting, however, and many Scots, whose political, professional, or social connections took them much to London, were painted by Reynolds (1723-1792), Gainsborough (1727-1788), or Romney (1734-1802). Nor were the minor London painters without their Scottish patrons: the number of fine Zoffanys (1733-1810), for instance, in Scotland is surprising. It was also the time of 'the grand tour,' and portraits by some of the Roman painters, and particularly by Pompeo Batoni (1702-1787), are to be found in many Scottish houses. To Batoni also are we indebted for that portrait which shows Prince Charles Edward as he was in his drunken and disreputable old age. And a sorry spectacle it is: the shadow side of that brilliant figure which bears itself so gallantly in the romantic halo that has gathered round the last attempt of the old line of Scottish kings to regain its forfeited place. But the 'Bonny Prince Charlie' of the happier time and of the Jacobite songs is best seen in the work of French hands, and specially in the bust by Lemoyne (1704-1778), which is at once the most pleasing and authentic portrait of the young Chevalier.

From such various sources it is possible to form a very complete notion of what the notable men and women of eighteenth-century Scotland were like. Here and there one is surprised that no portrait of some eminent person can be traced, but, on the whole, the blanks are fewer than one might expect. Of the philosophers, moral and natural, and of the poets and historians, who are the glory of Scotland in this century, there is a wonderfully complete series; and of most of the prominent actors in the '45 there are reliable portraits. But while many of these are by native artists, the art itself is marked by no very definitely Scottish characteristics. Most Scottish painters had studied abroad, and they were too few in number and too isolated to form a school. The characteristics of their portraiture in a technical sense were largely due to the masters and the schools with which they had been brought into contact. And yet within these acquired conventions there are often a shrewd reading of character and a simplicity and directness of statement, which indicate the nationality of the painter. Simplicity and freedom from affectation, a direct interest in the sitter as an individual, a preference for essentials rather than trappings, are what distinguished Jamesone and Wright, Aikman and Allan Ramsay at his best from their contemporaries in the south; and it was the possession of these qualities, and the power of expressing them in a masterly manner, that were to win Sir Henry Raeburn great fame.

Born in Edinburgh, Raeburn (1756-1828) was chiefly self-trained, and when, at the age of twenty-nine, he went to Rome, to study for two years, his style was practically formed. But wider experience enriched his art, while leaving it essentially unchanged, and within a few years he produced several masterpieces, which, in certain respects, remained unsurpassed by any subsequent achievement. It is to the last two decades of his career, however, that his most characteristic work belongs. In the bust and three-quarter lengths of that period he dispensed with conventionally artistic settings, and painted people simply and directly as they were. If he is less elegant in invention and design, and scarcely so good a colourist as Reynolds or Gainsborough, he gives a closer reading of character, and his portraitures are less marked by a preconceived and generalised type; and this, combined with his extraordinary gift of direct and unfaltering technical expression, gives his work a somewhat unique place in the British school, and in a wider survey almost justifies, that most subtle of critics, R. A. M. Stevenson's contention that it occupies the chief place between Velasquez and Hals and the modern schools in the development of direct painting. Belonging, as he undoubtedly does, and notably in treatment of light and values, and in the means used to concentrate attention, to the convention of the early British school, his interest in his sitter's personality and the directness of his method are essentially modern.

xvi

INTRODUCTION

It was a stroke of good fortune that he came when he did, for his brush has perpetuated in convincing fashion those who figured in the last brilliant epoch of distinctly Scottish national life, the period immediately preceding railways and steamers, and the closer contact with the sister country they brought. To name his sitters is to mention almost everybody of importance in his day. Burns excepted, no one of first-class interest seems to have escaped his brush.

The sober dignity, the masculine expressiveness, and the keen interest in character, which are so evident in his art, had been, to some extent, present in Scottish portraiture before his time; from it they may be said to have become its most obvious characteristics. George Watson (1767-1837), the first president of the Scottish Academy, and other of his immediate contemporaries, Andrew Geddes (1788-1844), Sir J. Watson Gordon (1788-1864), Graham Gilbert (1794-1866), Colvin Smith (1795-1875), and even Sir David Wilkie (1785-1841), as in the portrait of himself reproduced for this series, were influenced by his example, and to-day it still exists as a vital force in Scottish painting. Of those who were exclusively portrait-painters, Watson Gordon was the most important, and he did for the succeeding generation what Raeburn had done for their fathers. Less gifted technically, with less certainty in drawing and less gusto in handling, than his great predecessor, the best of his work possesses grave dignity of presentment, subtle strength of handling, and, now and then, a quiet charm of silvery tone and colour, which, united to a rare relish for character, in which shrewdness and humour are combined, give it enduring interest. He was, however, very distinctly a painter of men, and lacked that spontaneous appreciation of grace and abandon so essential to success in painting women and children. But, in his own field, he produced many fine things, amongst which the portrait of 'The Ettrick Shepherd,' painted for the proprietor of 'Maga,' in the pages of which he was immortalised by 'Christopher North,' ranks very high. If Andrew Geddes was not so much of a specialist, his finest pictures are probably portraits. To him we owe what is perhaps the most convincing, as it is certainly the most artistic, portrait of Sir Walter Scott, while those of his mother, in the National Gallery of Scotland, of Skirving the painter in his old age, and of Wilkie and Sicily Brydone, the last two cabinet pieces with a genre touch in them, are worthy to rank with the finest works of his school. Moreover, he was a fine colourist, and designed with simplicity and grace. He is also to be credited with a series of etchings, mostly figure studies and portraits, of real charm.

Turning now to those with whom portraiture was the exception rather than the rule, one finds that admirable work was done by Thomas Duncan (1807-1845) in such things as the autograph portrait, which was purchased by fifty of his fellow-artists after his too early death and presented to the Gallery on the Mound, or the wonderful likeness of Dr. Chalmers, which represents him here; by William Dyce (1806-1864), who attained in some of his portraits of children a beauty and charm not to be found in his more ambitious and better known religious pictures and mural decorations; and by Robert Scott Lauder (1803-1869), whose unique success as a master has overshadowed his considerable achievement as a painter. Lauder's pupils, who are as remarkable for versatility of subject as for artistic talent, included several who have painted portraits with more than usual charm. Mention of G. P. Chalmers (1833-1878) and John Pettie (1839-1893), of Mr. Orchardson and Mr. M'Taggart, will indicate at once the variety of their motives, and serve as a reminder of their success in portraiture.

Alongside these younger men Sir Daniel Macnee (1806-1882), whose incomparable gift of story-telling is fondly remembered by men not yet much past middle age, carried on the tradition of an older generation. An early member of the Scottish Academy, he had been a friend of Graham Gilbert, Geddes, and Horatio Macculloch, and, at his best, he almost deserves the compliment implied in describing him as 'an understudy of Raeburn.' But, for the most part, his best was confined to the forties and fifties, and if from time to time he continued to produce a portrait worthy of his talent, on the whole, his later work is more likeness-making than art. With him, but on a lower plane, may be bracketed a president of the London Academy, Sir Francis Grant (1803-1878), Norman Macbeth, R.S.A. (1821-1888), and a few more of similar tendencies. In these it may not be fanciful to trace the influence of photography with its close rendering of certain aspects of reality. Yet photography was introduced into Scotland by a painter and a photographer, who in collaboration achieved highly artistic results. The calotypes of D. O. Hill, R.S.A., for, while one does not forget Robert Adamson's share in them, the charm of these photographs belong to him, are indeed almost the most beautiful things ever obtained by the aid of a camera, and I make no apology for including that of Hugh Miller in this series of Scottish portraits. If by no means the best of Hill's calotypes, it is a fair

INTRODUCTION

average example, and it is perhaps the finest portrait of the author of *The Old Red Sandstone* and *My Schools and Schoolmasters* extant. While the sweeping claims for photography to rank as an art may be disputed, there is no doubt of the beauty of prints such as Hill's, and in any case photography has added greatly to the sources of portraiture as an historical document. To one branch of portrait-painting, however, the advent of the photograph gave the *coup de grâce*. Miniature, in which several Scottish painters had attained distinction, became a thing of the past, and Robert Thorburn (1818-1885), Kenneth Macleay (1802-1878), and others had to turn their talents into other channels.

Thirty or forty years before this the miniature in relief, in which the Tassies and John Henning (1771-1851) had done so much valuable portraiture, had come to an end; but about the same time portrait-sculpture in the round commenced to show some vitality in Scotland, principally in the artistic busts of Samuel Joseph, an Englishman long resident in Edinburgh, while Chantrey modelled several remarkably fine busts and statues of distinguished Scots. Since then sculpture has contributed much to the portraiture of Scotland. Sir John Steell (1804-1891), who is in a sense the father of Scottish sculpture, and whose statue of Provost Blaikie in Aberdeen is said to be the first marble statue ever carved in Scotland, left a whole gallery of busts, while James Fillans (1808-1852), Patrick Park (1809-1855), and the Brodies, to name the more conspicuous of the dead, did worthy work.

But, although for a century and more there has been a constant choice of good and sometimes fine portrait-artists in Scotland, 'far-away birds have fine feathers,' and a good many Scots have been painted by alien hands. This wider choice has resulted in notable contributions to art as well as portraiture, as in the case of some Lawrences, Watts, and Millais, Whistlers and Sargents, one could name, but not infrequently, choice being determined more often by popular or fashionable vogue than by artistic merit, with no such success as justifies the complaint that many of the best commissions go to London.

The definite power of artistic portraiture that has been noted in Scottish painting in the past continues unabated in the best of to-day, and the work of Mr. Orchardson and Sir George Reid, and of a number of younger men in London or at home, takes a high place in contemporary art. This, however, is not the place to discuss it; but as regards the younger school, the presence of Mr. Whistler's 'Carlyle' in the Glasgow Art Galleries may be taken as significant of the influences that have moulded it, and of the ideals to which it aspires.

SCOTTISH PORTRAITS

The sources of Scottish portraiture and its characteristics, in so far as it has been produced by Scotsmen, having been indicated, it remains to add something about the interest that has been taken in the subject itself. That in a general and historical sense is of comparatively recent origin. Before the middle of the eighteenth century, one might say that the interest in portraiture was personal and family. Then, as with us in connection with portraits of contemporaries, questions of art apart, the portrait of a man or a woman was mainly of interest to those of his own house. Portraits of Royalties were an exception, however, and seem always to have been in request. Thus in 1684 the Government contracted with James de Witt, a Flemish painter, to paint, for the miserly sum of £240—he supplying canvas and colours—one hundred and ten portraits of Kings and Queens of Scotland, from Fergus I. to James VII., to adorn the long gallery in Holyrood. To about the same period, also, one may assign the series of portraits of divines in Glasgow University: they are probably those copies of portraits of distinguished men for which John Scougall was paid a guinea apiece. But no real interest was taken in portraiture for its own sake or as an adjunct to history. Fortunately, however, replicas of portraits were painted frequently for people in the family connection, and a few men seem to have collected portraits of their friends or of distinguished contemporaries, while portrait-engravings, usually from pictures but occasionally from life, were rather in fashion, and now form a most valuable auxiliary to other sources of reliable portraiture. During the eighteenth century, greater, but often indiscriminating and uncritical, interest was aroused. In England the enthusiasm and knowledge of George Vertue (1684-1756) were devoted to the engraving and investigation of many historical portraits, and with the advent of Horace Walpole (1717-1797), who incorporated Vertue's notes in his *Anecdotes of Painting in England* (1762-1780), and other collectors, and specially of the Rev. James Granger (1723-1776), whose industry in collecting prints to illustrate English history resulted in the verb 'to Grangerise,' and in his valuable list of portrait-engravings, known as *A Biographical History of England* (1769), this interest became widely diffused. David, 'the daft' Earl of Buchan (1742-1829), seems to have aspired to the part of a Scottish Horace Walpole, but he was too erratic, fanciful, and credulous to be a safe guide, and an amusing and witty, but quite unprintable, epigram of Charles Kirkpatrick Sharpe's hits off his relationship to Scottish historical portraits very neatly. Yet the influence of his example, combined with that of the English enthusiasts, was largely responsible

INTRODUCTION

for the demand for portraits of the more notable personages of Scottish history, which became fashionable in the latter half of the eighteenth century. To meet this demand a supply was speedily forthcoming, and a regular trade was done in spurious 'originals' and in genuine old works rebaptized. But awakened interest brought other and more careful workers into the field, and Pinkerton's *Iconographia Scotica* (1797) and *Scottish Gallery* (1799), and Smith's *Iconographia* (1798), although containing a considerable proportion of doubtful portraits, are important contributions to the subject. A goodly number of Scots also found a place in Lodge's *Portraits of Illustrious Personages of Great Britain* (commenced 1814), a work of great value, in which Sir Walter Scott (1771-1832) naturally took a lively interest. But the value of the reproductions in these series of portraits is to a certain extent discounted by the process, for the finer points of likeness suffer even at a good engraver's hands, and the engravers employed by Pinkerton and Smith, at least, were not masters of their craft. Besides they usually worked from drawings made by others, and did not see the pictures for themselves. A more critical spirit and greater knowledge was brought to bear on the subject by C. K. Sharpe (1781-1851), Dr. David Laing (1790-1878), James Drummond, R.S.A. (1816-1877), and Sir William Stirling Maxwell (1818-1878), while the fervid, if uncritical, enthusiasm of Thomas Carlyle (1795-1881) gave a great impetus to study.

What seems to have been the first exhibition of Scottish historical portraits was held in Aberdeen, three years after the foundation of the National Portrait Gallery, London (1856), and, although small in numbers, it consisted of interesting works. Many Scottish portraits were shown in the exhibitions of national portraits at South Kensington in the years 1866-7-8, and helped to foster interest in the historical aspect of portraiture and to clear up numerous doubtful points. These were followed by a large collection, principally of West country notables, in Glasgow in 1868, of which a valuable photographic record remains, and then, in 1888 and the following year, in prospect of the foundation of the Scottish National Portrait Gallery, exhibitions of great educative value were held in Edinburgh by the Board of Manufactures. The first offer (1882) of the then anonymous donor was of £10,000, on condition that Government gave a similar sum to aid in the formation of a Scottish National Portrait Gallery; and, that being acceded to, the same gentleman offered to provide a building to house the Portrait Gallery and the National Museum of Antiquities, if the Government and the Board of Manufactures would find a suitable site. In 1889 the building in Queen Street, designed by Dr. Rowand Anderson, was far enough advanced to permit the removal of such portraits as had been acquired in the interval, and, at the formal opening, it was announced that the founder was Mr. J. R. Findlay of Aberlour and *The Scotsman*, who, some seven years later, gave a further sum to adorn the central hall with decorative pictures from Scottish history, and to complete the architecture by filling the niches on the exterior with statues of illustrious Scots. While Mr. Findlay spent over £70,000 on this institution, Government has voted only £15,000 in all, of which £10,000 added to the £10,000 originally gifted by the donor and invested in gilt-edged securities, provides the only income of the gallery, which, unlike that in London, has no annual grant. Yet, notwithstanding these most meagre resources, the generosity of private individuals and the tact and skill of the first curator, J. M. Gray (1850-1894), have resulted in the gathering together in the Queen Street gallery of a highly interesting collection of portraits illustrative of the history of Scotland. Since the foundation of the gallery the interest in Scottish historical portraiture has greatly increased. In such exhibitions as those in Glasgow in 1888 and 1901 the history section owed much of its charm to portraits, and the great advance in processes of reproduction has enabled portrait illustrations to historical and other works to become a feature of contemporary book-making. It remained, however, to bring together a collection of the best and most authentic portraits of the most famous Scots of the past, and that is the object of this work.

PORTRAITS

MARGARET OF AUSTRIA

KING JAMES III. OF SCOTLAND

1451-1488

MARGARET OF DENMARK

QUEEN OF JAMES III.

1457 ?–1486

Painter: Hugo Van der Goes (d. 1482).
Date: between 1473 and 1476.
Size: each panel, 82 × 44 ins.
In the possession of H.M. The King, by whose gracious permission
they are reproduced.

WHEN, on 3rd August 1460, James II. was killed, at the siege of
Roxburgh Castle, by the explosion of a bombard, his son and
heir was nine years old. Knowing the difficulties associated with
a minority in Scotland, the Queen, Mary of Gueldres, taking the prince with
her, hastened to the scene of action, and James III. was crowned at Kelso only
a week later. The Queen-Mother exercised considerable authority, but the
administration of the country lay principally with Bishop Kennedy of St. Andrews,
whose conduct of affairs was marked by notable success, especially after Mary's
death in 1463. But the Bishop died two years later, and thereafter the ground
was clear for the plottings of less capable and more self-seeking men. At
first the young King did not suffer, and in 1468, in order to settle a long-
standing difference between the countries, a marriage was arranged between
him and Margaret, daughter of Christian I., King of Denmark, Norway, and
Sweden. When, in July 1469, the marriage was celebrated with great
splendour at Holyrood, the King was in his eighteenth year, the bride in her
twelfth; and in 1473 they had a son, afterwards James IV., followed three
years later by a second, the Duke of Ross (1476-1504). The Queen was to
have brought a dowry of 60,000 florins and the cancellation of the annual
payment for the Western Isles, ceded by Norway to Alexander III., but, being

unable to raise more than 2000 florins, Christian pledged Orkney and Shetland against the remainder, and, failing to pay, these islands were annexed to Scotland in 1472. By 1478, when James took over the responsibility of government, the Orkney and Shetland Islands on the north, and Roxburgh and Berwick on the English border, had been added to his kingdom, and the Lord of the Isles had been subdued, while St. Andrews had been erected into an archiepiscopal see, so freeing the Scottish Church from the claims of the Archbishop of York; but soon the King's weakness as a ruler betrayed itself, and the rest of his career was a succession of difficulties with his brothers, with his nobles, and with England. Unlike his brothers, specially the Duke of Albany, who was an adept in all martial exercises, James preferred to cultivate the arts in the company of gifted but low-born favourites to fulfilling his duties as a feudal sovereign. The result was misunderstanding and jealousy, and in 1479 Albany and Mar were arrested. The former broke prison and escaped to France, where he won renown by his knightly skill; the latter died under circumstances which left a lasting stain on James's name. In 1482, during one of the recurrent disputes with England, the Scots King led an army towards the border, but the presence of his artistic favourites in the camp brought the discontent of the nobles to a head, and led by the Earl of Angus, who earned his well-known name, 'Bell the Cat,' on this occasion, they hung the favourites in a row over Lauder Bridge, and sent the King to Edinburgh Castle. But with the aid of Albany, who had been concerned covertly in the English actions that had led to the abortive campaign, and who was now alternately a seeming friend and an active traitor to his brother, he was restored to authority. Again the King's weak rule resulted in trouble, and the end came in 1488, when the more powerful of the Southern barons, placing the King's son at their head, broke into open revolt. James found strong support in the north, but when, on the 11th June, the armies met at Sauchieburn, the King fled while the issue was still doubtful, and taking refuge in Betoun's mill near by, was discovered and slain in cold blood—it is said by a soldier disguised as a priest—that evening. His Queen had died at Stirling two years before, and he was buried beside her in Cambuskenneth Abbey.

IN 1462 Queen Mary of Gueldres, consort of James II. of Scotland, founded the Collegiate Church of the Holy Trinity in Edinburgh, but no more than the choir and transepts had been built when the death of the foundress and, later, the Reformation intervened, and the edifice was never finished. The part completed was used, however, as a Presbyterian church until 1848, when, its site being scheduled for the Waverley Station, it was taken down, and served as a quarry for the present Trinity College Church in Jeffrey Street. A late but fine example of Gothic architecture, spared at the Reformation, was thus destroyed utterly for purely utilitarian reasons little more than fifty years ago. It was for this church that the altarpiece, of which the panels reproduced formed a part, was painted. No written record of its existence previous to the reign of James VI. and I. is known, and how it escaped the wholesale destruction of such things during the Reformation is matter for conjecture, although the fact that it contains portraits of several members of the Royal family is probably reason enough, if, as has been suggested, it was not carried to England amongst other plunder by the Earl of Hertford's expedition in 1544. But, as it does not appear in the inventories of Henry VIII.'s or Edward VI.'s pictures, it probably remained in Scotland until the Stuarts became Kings of England. It is first mentioned, 'Inprimis. King James the Third of Scotland with his Queene, doune by Joan Vanek' in 'A note of all such Pictures as your Highness (James I.) hath at the present, done by severall Famous Masters' owne hands, by the Life,' which is understood to have been compiled in October 1624; and, while it does not figure in the catalogue of Charles I.'s collection, it was at Hampton Court, Nos. 955 and 960, during the reign of James II. Thence, after being for some time at Kensington in the interval, it was transferred to Holyrood in 1857 by Queen Victoria. The altarpiece had been described, and three of its subjects engraved by Pinkerton (*Iconographia Scotica*, 1797), and it had been noticed by Dr. Waagen, by Passavant (*Tour of a German Artist in England*, 1836), and by Charles Blanc (*Les Trésors de l'Art à Manchester*, Paris, 1857); but it was David Laing, LL.D., who first investigated it minutely, and, if a few of his suppositions are erroneous or remain unproved, little of definite moment has since been added to his conclusions (see *Proceedings of the Society of Antiquaries of Scotland*, vols. iii. and x.).

The whole work, or at least all that remains of it, consists of two panels of fir, coated with gypsum and painted on both sides. One panel has on one side portraits of James III. of Scotland and his son, with St. Andrew; and on the other side a very striking representation of the Holy Trinity. The second has a portrait of James's Queen, Margaret of Denmark, with an armoured saint, either St. George or some unrecognised Danish saint; and on its reverse a portrait

3

of an ecclesiastic kneeling beside an organ which is being played by an angel, a second angel being in attendance. These panels are now arranged as two separate pieces, and, being placed on stands in the long gallery at Holyrood, all the faces can be examined.

From internal evidence the altarpiece, of which they formed parts, was gifted by Sir Edward Bonkil or Boncle, who is referred to repeatedly in the public records of the time, to Trinity College Church, of which he was the first provost; for, as is usual in votive pictures, he is represented in one of the compartments, and can be identified from his arms. The occasion of the gift has led to various suppositions, none of them very satisfactory; but that it was in some way connected with the royal marriage or the birth of an heir is probable enough. Pinkerton, who advanced no theory of origin, assumed that the prince in the King's compartment was his son (afterwards James IV.), aged from ten to twelve, and dated the picture about 1583, and, at first, Laing accepted these conclusions. Further consideration, however, induced him to modify this view. As the actual difference in age between James and his son was more than twenty years, and that indicated in the picture was far less, he decided that the prince was more probably the King's younger brother, the Duke of Albany (d. 1485), who fled to France and was forfeited in 1479. But this theory is open to the same objection: the apparent difference in age in the picture is greater than the three years there actually were between the King and Albany. More important still, it was the almost invariable custom to represent children and not brothers or sisters in such pictures, and as this altarpiece was probably painted in Flanders from material supplied by the donor, the apparent ages of King and prince are not of first-class importance. Moreover, the anomaly of representing even a very young prince as of older years is not unknown in fifteenth and sixteenth century art. In the votive picture of St. George and the Dragon, with kneeling figures of Henry VII., his Queen and children, in the Royal collection, the infant Catherine and the three-year-old Elizabeth are represented as well-grown girls, while Prince Edmund, who died at the age of one, looks almost as old as the prince in the Scottish picture. A similar liberty was taken in an old decoration, showing the family of King Edward III., in St. Stephen's Chapel, Westminster; and the sarcophagus of the Countess of Lenox (1515-1577) in the same abbey is surrounded by kneeling statues of her children as boys and girls, though most of them died in infancy. Everything considered, I am inclined to accept the traditional designation of the prince as James IV., and in that case the picture may be dated

KING JAMES III. AND MARGARET

definitely between 1478 and 1476. The King's second child was born in the latter year, and if painted later, following the artistic convention of the period, he also would have been introduced into the picture.

The suggestion that the saints and angels in the three panels in which they appear are portraits of other personages of the period is somewhat far fetched. With the St. Andrew and the uncertain armed saint who stands behind the kneeling Queen it has never gone beyond conjecture, but the attempt to identify the angel seated at the organ as Mary of Gueldres, who founded the church, was quite definite. But the wings of the musician are greatly against the probability of its being intended for a portrait at all, and the jewelled circlet on her head, which Pinkerton and Laing both thought to indicate a Royal personage, is to be seen also on certain of the angels in the Portinari altarpiece by Van der Goes at Florence, or on the singing and playing angels in the wings (now in Berlin), painted by the Van Eycks for their famous altarpiece in Ghent, where no such claim can be advanced.

Having indicated the personages represented and the probable date of painting, the next point to be considered is the probable arrangement of the panels. Dr. Laing thought that they were the wings of a three-compartment design of an architectural character, in which the central division would be formed by a carved crucifix or suchlike subject, and that the panels showing the King and Queen would face the church and the figures each other. This practice of combining painting and sculpture in an altarpiece is not unknown in both Netherlandish and Italian art, but there is nothing to show that such was the case here, and it is at least equally possible that, as in the triptych by Van der Goes already referred to, the central compartment was a picture, and, being of a purely religious nature, was destroyed during the Reformation. Some triple arrangement is most likely indeed, but Laing's suggested placing of the panels is open to a grave objection. Looking from behind the altar at the fixed arrangement first suggested by him, the pious donor, instead of adoring the 'Trinity,' would have been seen with his back turned upon it, while in the second, where he speaks of the panels as the folding-doors of a triptych, the King and Queen would have faced each other without an object of adoration between. But if the latter and usual course had been followed and the panels are the folding-wings of a triptych (the centre of which was either a sculptured or painted panel), another and perfectly satisfactory supposition for their arrangement is possible. If the 'Trinity' and Bonkil compartments had been the external faces of such an altarpiece, they would, when the doors were closed, have formed a related whole, the donor adoring the 'Holy Trinity,' to whom the church was dedicated, in much the same way as Joan de Bourbon adores the 'Crucifixion' in the diptych now at Chantilly, or Martin van Nieuwenhove the Madonna in the charming Memlinc in the Hôpital Saint-Jean at Bruges, while, when they were open, the King and Queen would have been seen facing each other and worshipping the central and more important object of adoration, which the doors, when closed, masked. Thus, closed or open, the altarpiece would have had a clear *raison d'être*.

The question of to whom this altarpiece should be attributed has been much discussed. The catalogue of James vi.'s pictures gives it to Van Eyck, but both brothers were dead before it could have been begun. Dr. Waagen and others assigned it to Jean Gossaert, usually called Mabuse, and that ascription has won considerable acceptance; and Passavant, without attributing it to Van der Goes, mentions that master's name in connection with it. Charles Blanc was more specific, and discussed it as a work of Van der Goes, and this ascription, which Dr. Laing in his second paper inclined to adopt, has tended to become more and more accepted. The letters 'PRAT' (the second is indefinite) upon the head-dress of the Queen have led to the conjecture that it might be the work of one, David or John, Pratt, whose name appears in connection with art-work done for James iv. at Stirling in 1497 and 1502. There is, however, nothing more to go upon, no authentic work of his having survived, and the lettering probably has no reference to the painter. Indeed, a queen's headdress would be a most unusual place for an artist to sign his name. Mabuse, to whom, as previously stated, it has been assigned frequently, was, if the prince represented is, as is most probable, James iv., too late to have painted it, and in addition the style of handling, drawing, and composition make it most unlikely that he had aught to do with it. It has also been suggested that two or more artists were engaged upon the work: that the inner panels of the King and Queen are by one hand, and the outer of Bonkil and the 'Holy Trinity' by another. Other critics have assigned the three portrait-panels to one painter and the 'Trinity' only to a second. The difference between the Bonkil and the King and Queen is, however, as great as that between the portrait-panels and the 'Trinity,' and probably the marked difference between the outer sides of the shutters, taken together or separately, and the inner ones, is due to the better condition of the latter, and this again is easily traceable to the subjects having led, since the Reformation, to their being less exposed than the Royal faces. Of all the panels the 'Trinity'

6

is best preserved, and has been least retouched. Comparing it with the Bonkil, one finds many technical resemblances of which the most notable is perhaps the way in which gilding is used. In both it is confined to a single great mass, in the 'Trinity' to the throne, in the Bonkil to the organ; and the modelling upon these is obtained by a hatch-work of lines, used in a somewhat similar way to pen-work in illumination. In all the panels no real gold is used on the personal ornaments or the dresses; on the outer faces it is confined to the objects mentioned, and in the inner to the heraldry. Perhaps the halos have been gilded also, but it is difficult to say definitely. Otherwise gold, as was usual in early Flemish work, is represented by painting. Again, comparing the 'Trinity' with the King's panel, which is most retouched of all, one may note the similarity in the handling and tones of the red and green robes, the resemblance between 'The Father' and the St. Andrew in type, and the fact that the halos (about the Queen's saint's head also) are represented by radial lines. The temper of conception in the 'Trinity,' it must be admitted, is of another order from that in the other panels, and the intensity of austerity in the 'Christ' reminds one forcibly of such things as Van der Weyden's 'Holy Sacrament' in Antwerp and 'Entombment' in the Uffizi; but much of this may be attributed to the conception prevalent amongst the earlier followers of the Van Eycks. Turning now to the difference between the Bonkil and the Royal compartments, it will be found chiefly in the portrait heads. Compared with the Royal personages, Bonkil is completely and powerfully realised; not only his head but his hands must have been painted from the life, while those of James and the Queen and the prince are somewhat empty and contain nothing that could not have been painted from drawings or other material supplied to the artist. The repainting that the King's face and hands have undergone is not sufficient to account for the greater power with which Bonkil is painted, and, as already suggested, the altarpiece was probably commissioned by the provost when on a visit to the Netherlands (where ecclesiastical fittings were often made for Scottish churches), and he himself painted from life. Another point, not without bearing on this supposition, is that the heads of the saints, beside whom the Royalties kneel, are far more fully modelled and searchingly drawn than those of the worshippers. On the whole, therefore, probability and the weight of evidence are in favour of the altarpiece being the work of one man, and, for reasons previously stated, of its having been painted between 1478 and 1476.

Of all the artists of his school then painting, Hugo Van der Goes seems the most likely to have executed these panels. His work is exceedingly rare, for, while a number of galleries contain pictures or portraits attributed to him, the famous Portinari altarpiece, now in the picture-gallery of the Hospital of S. Maria Nuova, Florence, which is mentioned by Vasari, and is dated by M. Wauters 1470-5, seems the only one upon the authenticity of which experts agree. This the Holyrood pictures resemble in many ways. The general arrangement is very similar, but that, of course, conforms to the usual type and means nothing. But the scale of both—the wings of the Florence picture are each 5·85 by 101 inches, the Holyrood panels each 44 by 82 inches, or a ratio of 1·88 and 1·86 respectively—is greater than usual; the drawing and the pose of the heads and figures of the worshippers is similar in style; the management of the draperies, in which the folds are simpler than is usual in Flemish painting, is much alike; the younger saint in the left panel of the Portinari piece is exceedingly like the St. Andrew in type, and might almost have been painted from the same model; one of the Portinari boys resembles the Scots prince closely; the type of angel in both has considerable resemblance. So much is apparent from a careful comparison of photographs, and, although the lavish use of gilding in the Holyrood panels, the difference in the character of the backgrounds, and a certain amount of repainting in both present difficulties, those who have examined the originals see resemblances in the technique and colour. Moreover, the discrepancy in temper between the 'Trinity' and the portrait parts of the Holyrood pictures accords with what is known of this master. M. Wauters, who has studied his work more closely, perhaps, than any other European critic, has singled out a combination of austerity and grace as specially characteristic of his talents. From 1478 to 1475 Van der Goes was dean of the Guild of Painters in Ghent, and in 1476 he made a sudden retreat to the monastery of Rouge-Cloître, where he continued to work at his art, with occasional lapses into drink or madness, until his death in 1482. During the time this picture was most probably painted, Van der Goes was available for such commissions, and, everything considered, it is likely that the Holyrood altarpiece is the work of his hands. Yet all that can be said certainly is that it is more probably by him than by any of his known contemporaries of the Flemish school of the fifteenth century, to some great master of which it indubitably belongs.

8

KING JAMES IV.
1473 - 1513
PAINTING BY THOMAS NICHOLS

PLATE III
KING JAMES IV. OF SCOTLAND
1473–1513

Painter: DANIEL MYTENS (1590?-1642), after an older portrait.
Size: 37 × 24 ins.
In the possession of ARCHIBALD STIRLING, Esq. of Keir.

THE eldest son of James III. was born on 17th March 1473, and was only fifteen when his father's rebel lords placed him at the head of the revolt which ended in the King's murder after the battle of Sauchieburn, 11th June 1488. He was crowned before the month was out, and the great offices of state passed into the hands of the leaders of the late rebellion. The earlier years of his reign were divided amongst projects of marriage, expeditions against the turbulent Island chiefs, and fighting on the English border, the latter in part on behalf of the pretender, Perkin Warbeck. At length, after protracted negotiations, initiated by Henry VII., a marriage was arranged between his daughter, the Princess Margaret Tudor, and the King of Scots. On the 8th August 1503 the wedding took place at Holyrood amid great rejoicings, which are mirrored in Dunbar's famous poem, 'The Thistle and the Rose,' and, exactly a century later, the long-sighted policy of the English King resulted in the union of the crowns in the person of the great-grandson of the marriage. Peace with England enabled James to give his energies to important reforms in law and education, to the administration of justice and the formation of a navy, which, under the able captains, Sir Andrew Wood of Largo and the Bartons, reached a high state of efficiency. Moreover, he played a greater part in European politics than any of his predecessors, and his friendship was sought and valued by Pope and kings. The death of his father-in-law, however, and the formation of the Holy League against France, which left that country Scotland as her sole ally, now complicated Scottish affairs, and the difference with England was exaggerated through a quarrel between the Scots queen and her brother, Henry VIII. Henry's refusal to desist from war with France, combined with an appeal from the French queen, precipitated events, and the Scots army, 80,000 strong, marched into Northumberland. Norham and Wark and

B
9

Ford Castles were taken; but James, charmed by the beauty of Lady Heron, wasted precious days, and the English army approached the Border. Surrey sent a herald proposing battle for 9th September 1513, and, with an excess of chivalry, James consented; but, being out-generalled in the preliminary movements, had to change his position at the last moment. The battle that followed was long and stubborn and bloody. When darkness fell the Scots still faced the enemy, but before day broke they had fled. The King, most of his chief nobles, and ten thousand men were slain:

'The Flowers of the Forest are a' wede away.'

Flodden was the greatest disaster Scotland had known, but Surrey's force was so far spent that he could not follow up his advantage by crossing Tweed.

PEDRO D'AYALA, a Spanish envoy to Scotland in 1496 and 1497, seems to have been greatly charmed by the King, and his reports to his Government give quite a glowing account of both King and country. 'The King is twenty-five years and some months old. He is of noble stature, neither tall nor short, and as handsome in complexion and shape as a man can be. His address is very agreeable. He never cuts his hair or beard. It becomes him well' (Despatch to Ferdinand and Isabella, 25th July 1498). This contemporary account of James's appearance has been used to throw doubt on the authenticity of his portraits, which show him clean shaven. Ayala's description is further confirmed by one of the English heralds who was present at the royal marriage in 1503, and remarks on the length of the royal beard. But these records, true at the time they were written, are not the last word. An entry in the Lord High Treasurer's accounts, dated the day after the wedding, tells of the cutting of the King's beard, and as he was much older than his bride, it is not assuming much to imagine that the intention was to make the bridegroom more youthful in appearance. Judging from the payment, it was no ordinary clipping. The entry in the ledger runs:

'Item. The ix day of August, after the marige, for xv elne claith of gold to the Countess of Sury of Ingland, quhen scho and hir dochter Lady Gray clippit the Kingis berd ilk elne xxij. Item for xv elne damas gold be the Kingis command to the said Lady Gray of Ingland ilk elne xij.'

From the cutting of the never cut beard to a shaven face is but a step, and that step is taken in James's best authenticated portrait. One of a series of copies of older portraits, painted by Daniel Mytens for King James VI., this

10

picture is entered in the catalogue of Charles First's pictures at Whitehall (1639) as No. 15 in the Bear Garden. ' Item. Beside the door, the picture of King James IV. of Scotland, with a faulcon on his fist, done after an ancient water-colour piece, half a figure so big as the life, in a carved frame.' The ' ancient water-colour piece' referred to was probably a tempera picture on panel, and almost certainly the portrait mentioned in inventories of the English Royal collections drawn up in 1542-7 and 1548 or 1549 as ' Jacobbe Kynne of Skottes, with a hawke on his fiste, protected by a curtain,' and ' Item, a table with the picture of Jacobus quartus Rex Scotorum.' In the former case it was at Westminster, in the latter at St. James's. The Mytens portrait seems to have been in James II.'s collection at Whitehall, and probably fell into private hands after the fire there in 1697. When Pinkerton had it engraved for his *Iconographia*, it belonged to Mr. Batsford, at Fulham. It was acquired by Sir William Stirling-Maxwell, and is now in the possession of his son, Mr. Stirling of Keir. In the picture his eyes are greyish hazel, represented by neutral grey within a rim of yellow, and his long hair is brown; he wears a red mantle trimmed with leopard's skin, and the slashes show cloth of gold; the cap is black, with an *enseigne*. A falcon sits on his left hand, and he holds the lilac and green hood in his right. In each spandrel of the ruddy-brown archway is a rampant unicorn holding a shield, upon which the bearings are almost obliterated; below one is ' J,' below the other ' IV,' and across the top, in Gothic lettering, is ' In my defens.'

Of the other portraits of James IV., a drawing preserved in the Bibliothèque of the town of Arras in France, by a French or Flemish artist of the sixteenth century (perhaps Jacques Le Boucq of Artois), most closely resembles the Keir portrait in facial type and in the manner in which the hair is worn, and, although the costume and action are different, they may well derive from one source. Owing to much retouching, the portrait at Newbattle Abbey can be spoken of less certainly, but the fairish hair does not increase one's belief in it, and technically it is later than Flodden. The daisy, held in one hand, has been supposed to allude to his wife's name, but it appears in other pictures of the period where no such allusion is possible. An interesting portrait, dated 1507, showing a man not unlike James in type, belonged to Sir Walter Scott. It was presented to him by Archibald Constable, his publisher, and is still at Abbotsford. Not improbably it represents him. Johnston's *Inscriptiones* (1602) also shows him with beardless face and long hair.

PLATE IV

MARGARET TUDOR

QUEEN OF JAMES IV.

1489–1541

Painter: JEAN GOSSAERT, commonly called MABUSE (1470?-1532).
Date: unknown.
Size: panel 28½ × 21½ ins.
In the Scottish National Portrait Gallery.

MARGARET, the eldest daughter of Henry VII., King of England, was born at Westminster on 29th November 1489, and, in happy augury, was baptized on the following, St. Andrew's, day. In fulfilment of a long-cherished design of her father's, who saw in it the possibilities of union, she was betrothed, in January 1502, to King James IV. of Scotland, and the marriage was celebrated in Edinburgh in August of the following year, the King being in his thirty-first, and his bride in her fourteenth year. After four years she had a son, but he died in infancy, as did the next two children. In 1512, however, a son, who survived and became James V., was born. During James's life the Queen took little part in public affairs, but she seems to have sided with her husband against her brother, Henry VIII., in the events which preceded Flodden, and by his will she was left Regent of the country and guardian of her son. But the country was divided, and she was unable to prevent the recall of the Duke of Albany, a cousin of the late King's and son of the Duke who had been traitor to James III. Nor was her position strengthened by her sudden marriage with the Earl of Angus, a youth of less than twenty; and, Albany having arrived and been elected Regent, she fled to England, where she gave birth to a daughter, afterwards Countess of Lenox and mother of Lord Darnley. In 1517, during Albany's long absence in France, she came to Scotland again, and on his return they were reconciled, and he and she were even charged with being 'over tender.' Meanwhile she was working in the English interest, and trying to get divorce from Angus, succeeding in which

12

MARGARET QUEEN OF JAMES IV.
(1489-1541)

she immediately married another young man, Henry Stewart of the Evandale family. When, little more than a year later, her son secured liberty of action and Angus fled to England, Margaret and her husband, who was created Lord Methven, were received into great favour, but she lost much of her influence through sending secret information to England. Tiring of Methven, she would have divorced him also, had her son not interfered. In 1541 she died, and was buried, as she would have wished, splendidly in St. John's Church, Perth.

Fickle and vain and wilful, unscrupulous and lustful, she was, although much less able and intelligent, not unlike her brother in temperament and, in her later years, in person also. The brightest spots in her career were her patronage of William Dunbar and her friendship for Gawain Douglas, for whom she secured the bishopric of Dunkeld.

WHILE no portrait of Margaret Tudor can be traced right back to her day, the full-length at Hampton Court, which formed one of the series of portraits of his ancestors painted for King James VI. by Daniel Mytens, from originals now lost, supplies an adequate test for portraits claiming to represent her. The features and colouring in that canvas are clearly marked, and, judged by it, there are several pictures of contemporary workmanship which conform to the type so closely that they may be accepted. Chief amongst these is the panel picture by Mabuse in the Scottish National Portrait Gallery, which, after being for something approaching a century and a half in the well-known collection at Lee Priory, Kent, was purchased by Sir Hugh Hume Campbell of Marchmont, who bequeathed it to the Edinburgh Gallery. With round pink face, lustrous brown hair, soft brown eyes, rich red lips, and a suggestion of a *petite*, if rather full, figure, it is easily accepted as Margaret Tudor at a rather earlier age than in the Mytens portrait. When she was very young, Ayala, the Spanish ambassador, remarked that she was small for her age, and Gawain Douglas speaks of her bright complexion and abundant golden hair. In the Introduction the difficulty of fitting the Queen's movements to those of the painter, if he was never (Van Mander says he was) in this country, has been discussed, and here it is sufficient to repeat that it is all but certainly by him, and a portrait of her.

A celebrated little picture (panel 18¾ × 11 ins.) in Lord Lothian's collection at Newbattle has also been accepted as a portrait of Margaret, when she had grown fat. The type conforms to that in the portraits already mentioned, but

13

the eyes are grey. It is assigned to Holbein, but in addition to a difficulty of dates there is one of style. A French painter of the school of Clouet would probably be a more likely attribution: the drawing, handling, and colour remind one vividly of the charming little portrait of Francis II. as a child in the Antwerp Gallery. There is a drawing resembling this closely in the Lenoir collection, now at Chantilly. It is reproduced in Lord Ronald Gower's lithographs, and J. M. Gray suggested, in his notes on the Newbattle collection, that it might even be a study for the Lothian picture. This is not improbable. The drawing in the Arras library shows a much thinner woman, and is rather out of line with the general type of Margaret's portraits. At Cardiff Castle there is another portrait in a group with the Duke of Albany and a herald or a servant, painted in satire, it is thought, about the time she and the Regent were accused of being over tender. That picture (panel 82½ × 45½) was minutely described and analysed by Sheriff Mackay in a paper which appears in the *Transactions of the Scottish Society of Antiquaries* (1892-8), where it is illustrated. According to Mr. Mackay it probably passed into Lord Bute's possession from the Windsor family, but Pinkerton, who had it engraved for his *Scottish Gallery* (1799), states that it formerly belonged to the Earl of Scarborough. This is confirmed by a letter of Walpole's to Sir David Dalrymple (Feb. 10, 1781). 'There is,' he writes, 'at Lord Scarborough's in Yorkshire a double portrait (perhaps by Holbein or Lucas de Heere) of Lady Margaret's mother, Queen Margaret, and her second husband.' Her second husband was the Earl of Angus, but it is clearly demonstrated in the article referred to that it is Albany who is represented. While the Queen's face is less plump and pleasing in this rendering, it possesses a considerable resemblance to the others. A few years ago a portrait attributed to the school of Bernard van Orley was added to the London Portrait Gallery. It resembles the Hampton Court and Edinburgh portraits in form, and has the same colour of hair and eyes.

PLATE V

WILLIAM ELPHINSTONE

BISHOP OF ABERDEEN

1431–1514

Painter: WILLIAM OF BRUGES.
Size: 26¼ × 20¼ ins.
In the possession of LORD ELPHINSTONE.

OF doubtful, and perhaps illegitimate, parentage, William Elphinstone was born in Glasgow, and, educated at the college there (M.A. 1452), continued his studies in Paris, where he was appointed 'first reader' in canon law. Later he lectured in the University of Orleans on the same subject. He was already in Holy Orders, and on returning to Scotland he began to take a prominent part in ecclesiastical and state affairs. After various lesser preferments he was consecrated (1484) Bishop of Aberdeen, where, having obtained a bull from Pope Alexander VI., he founded a University and built King's College, which under his care and that of Hector Boece, whom he appointed rector, became the most efficient in the kingdom. He had also to do with the establishment of the first printing-press in Scotland. As a statesman he was engaged in many negotiations and embassies, and in 1488 he was appointed Lord High Chancellor of the kingdom, but did not retain that office after Sauchieburn. In 1492, however, he was made Keeper of the Privy Seal, a post he seems to have held until his death. In foreign relationships he favoured agreement with England rather than the French alliance, and, in both church and state, he is accounted one of the greatest figures of his age and country.

BISHOP ELPHINSTONE'S likeness is preserved in two versions of one portrait. That in the University he founded is contemporary, but it hangs in shreds from the panel on which it was painted; the other, that reproduced, is old also, and has been in the possession of his family at Carberry Tower time out of mind. It is attributed to William of Bruges, whose identity cannot be established, and is probably a work of the Flemish school. Although somewhat repainted, it is in fair condition. The Aberdeen authorities had their original copied (canvas 80 × 25 ins.) by James Wales (1747-95). In it gold has been used, but there is none in Lord Elphinstone's picture, which bears the bishop's arms and initials and the inscription, 'William Elphinstone, Bishop of Aberdeen and Lord Chancellor of Scotland, Na. 1431, Ob. 1514,' in the upper left corner. Probably this inscription is a later addition. The Aberdeen portrait has no inscription, and the arms, with the motto 'Non Confundar' printed on a ribbon below them, are placed lower on the canvas. Instead of a plain background a curtain is looped up in the right upper corner, and through a window on the left is a glimpse of river landscape with shipping. The face in the Aberdeen copy is younger and less worn than in the Carberry picture.

PLATE VI

KING JAMES V. AND MARY OF GUISE

JAMES V., 1512–1542
MARY OF GUISE, 1515–1560

Painter : unknown.
Date : 1540.
Size : panel 43 × 56¾ ins.
In the possession of the DUKE OF DEVONSHIRE, K.G.

A S James v. was only seventeen months old when he succeeded his
father, his minority was one of the longest of the many in Scottish
history. As usual, it was a time of constant contests for power
amongst the more ambitious and powerful of the nobles and clergy, while the
prostration of the country after Flodden left it peculiarly open to attack. Fortunately, however, the attention of Henry VIII. was occupied otherwise, and,
despite Border bickerings, no open breach with England took place till 1528.
In 1526 James was assigned the Royal authority, but his step-father, the Earl
of Angus, controlled his actions, and it was not until two years later that he
succeeded in freeing himself. The King's first task was to break the Douglas
power and to secure order on the Borders and in the Islands, and in doing this
he alienated many of his barons, and came to rely for support principally on the
clergy and the people. To the former he was a good son of the Church, and
sought to suppress heresy; with the latter 'the Gude Man of Ballangeich' was
exceedingly popular. In 1537 marriage with Madeleine, daughter of Francis I.,
leagued him definitely with France, and when, a few months later, the fragile
but beautiful Queen died, he found (1538) a second consort in Marie, eldest
daughter of the Duke of Guise and widow of the Duc de Longueville, whose
sympathies were naturally strongly in favour of Catholicism and the French
alliance. The influence of Cardinal Beaton, now risen to great power, told in

the same direction, and it was friendship for France that at length ended the strained relations with England in the war that issued, on 24th November 1542, in the rout of Solway Moss, a disgraceful disaster, which so preyed on the King's mind that he died at Falkland on the 14th December. Only a week before, a daughter, afterwards Queen Mary, had been born at Linlithgow, but all he said, when the news was brought, was, 'The devil go with it. It will end as it began. It came with a lass, and it will go with a lass.'

The Queen's influence had been considerable in James's lifetime, and now he was dead she became the head of the French party in Scotland, and induced the nobles to betroth the young Queen to the Dauphin and send her to France. When her daughter reached the age of twelve, the Queen-Mother was appointed governor of Scotland, and sought to conduct its affairs on lines suggested by her brothers, the Duke of Guise and the Cardinal of Lorraine. During her regency the Reformation came to a head rapidly, and she had great trouble with the Lords of the Congregation, who were gaining the ascendency when she died, 11th June 1560.

AS an inscription upon the picture, which is a contemporary work, gives the ages of the King and Queen as twenty-eight and twenty-four respectively, it must have been painted between April and November 1540, and, with other Stuart portraits, it is mentioned in an old catalogue of the Harwick pictures compiled, probably, about the time of the death of the celebrated ' Bess of Harwick' (1518-1608), wife of the Earl of Shrewsbury (1528?-1590), who was Mary Queen of Scots' keeper during the first sixteen years she was in England. It is possible, therefore, that this portrait of Mary's father and mother may have come to Harwick during her imprisonment there. The arms upon it are— above, the Royal Arms of Scotland circled with the collar, bearing the jewel of St. Andrew; and, below, Scotland impaled with Lorraine, with a unicorn and an eagle for supporters. A second portrait in the same collection—a 8 ft. 6 in. full-length—has been supposed to represent James in his youth; but the costume is far too late, and it may be a likeness of his grandson, James VI. In the Royal Collection at Windsor there is an admirable half-length (panel $20\frac{1}{4} \times 15\frac{1}{2}$ ins.) of James V., which closely resembles the Harwick picture in likeness, but differs from it in pose and costume. It was probably in Charles I.'s collection. The Scottish National Portrait Gallery has an inferior version of the Harwick type

KING JAMES V. AND MARY OF GUISE

(panel 36 × 24 ins.), and a smaller one (panel 20 × 18 ins.), in which the figure is turned in the opposite direction. The last resembles the small panel (14 × 10 ins.) which belongs to the Castle Fraser family, but in it he does not wear the collar and badge of St. Andrew.

All these portraits agree in the form of the King's features, and in the ruddy, almost chestnut, hair and beard, which appear to have earned him the name of 'The Red Toad' (or Fox); but there is a discrepancy in the colour of the eyes, the Harwick picture showing them distinctly brown, that at Windsor blue-grey, and the others inclining to a greyish-hazel. His contemporary, Buchanan, describes him as of middle height, strong and graceful figure, and handsome countenance; and Bishop Leslie, who, if he never saw James, knew scores of people who had, records that his eyes were grey and keen.

Although Sir George Scharf's great authority was given in support of the portrait titled Mary of Lorraine in the London Portrait Gallery, which once belonged to Mr. Fraser Tytler, the historian, who called it Mary Queen of Scots, it is difficult to accept his conclusions. Tytler bought it of a dealer, Gwennap, who had acquired it from a portrait-painter named Stewart. Its previous history is unknown, but it may be accepted as the work of a French painter of the latter half of the sixteenth century. On the strength of its unlikeness, in some respects, to Mary Stuart, its arms, monogram, and background, and because it possessed a certain resemblance to the authentic portrait of Mary of Guise at Harwick, Sir George thought it a portrait of the latter, painted about the close of her life. But, as the Queen-Mother was then forty-five years of age, and much worn by disease, and the London portrait represents a fresh young woman, this is almost impossible. The dress, also, specially the type of ruff, belongs to some years later, as may be seen by comparison with the splendid lithographs in Neil's series of French portraits, or with the drawings reproduced by Lord Ronald Sutherland Gower, while the arms, motto, and monogram could apply equally and more appropriately to her daughter, for whom the costume would be quite suitable. These considerations, combined with the fact that the face in the Harwick picture, painted when Mary of Guise was twenty-four, is at once older and more marked in type, with more prominent cheekbones, a sharper nose, and a narrower and more projecting chin, make one hesitate to accept it as a portrait of her. On the other hand, I am disposed to regard it as a contemporary portrait of her daughter; but, the colour of hair and

19

eyes being wrong, and the likeness unconvincing, not painted from life. One is therefore again reduced to the position that the only authentic portrait of Mary of Guise is that reproduced. In it she has a fair complexion, grey eyes, and reddish hair and eyebrows; her elaborate cap of yellow and red is ornamented with jewels; her dress is brown, richly flowered with gold, her sleeves are ermine; and the carnation she holds is pink and white. No gilding is used, the gold being represented by paint.

PLATE VII

GEORGE WISHART

1513 ?–1546

Painted in the style of HOLBEIN.
Date: 1543.
Size: oak panel 23½ × 17½ ins.
In the Scottish National Portrait Gallery.

A CADET of the Pitarrow family, George Wishart seems to have been a graduate of Aberdeen, but little is known of his early life except that he taught Greek in Montrose, and, being accused of heresy, sought refuge in England, where his beliefs were again challenged. A visit to the Continent followed, and then, after residing for a time at Cambridge, where he became a member of Corpus Christi College, he returned to Scotland. There he devoted himself to preaching, principally at Montrose and Dundee, where he laboured zealously during the plague; in Ayrshire, where the influence of the Lollards of Kyle still lingered; and latterly, in the Lothians, where he met John Knox. His preaching convinced and converted many, and his saintly life was a constant reproach to the Catholic clergy, so, after several attempts to have him removed by assassination, he was arrested, at the instance of Cardinal Beaton, and carried captive to St. Andrews, where he was tried by a convocation of bishops and clergy and condemned to death. On March 1, 1546, he was burned at the stake before the castle of St. Andrews, the Cardinal looking on.

A LETTER of Emery Tylney's, one of his pupils at Cambridge, gives a vivid sketch of Wishart's personal appearance and character. 'About the year of our Lord, a thousand, five hundreth, forty and three, there was in the University of Cambridge, one Maister George Wishart, commonly called Maister George of Bennet's Colledge, who was a tall man, polde headed, and on the same a round French cap of the best. Judged of melancholye complexion by his physiognomie; black-haired, long bearded, comely of personage, well spoken after his country of Scotland, courteous, lowly, lonely, glad to teach, desirous to learne, and was well travailed. Having on him for his habit or clothing never but a mantill frieze gowne to the shoes, a black milliard fustian dublet, and plain black hosen, coarse new canvasse for his shirtes, and white falling bandes and cuffes at the hands. . . . He was a man, modest, temperate, fearing God, hating covetousnese; for his charitie had never ende, night, noone nor daye.' And with this description the portrait reproduced agrees closely. The only difference seems in the colour of the sleeves of the doublet, which are rather very dark brown than black in the picture; the 'falling bandes' mentioned in the description are traceable below the repainting the figure has undergone. Yet retouched, and in several places repainted as the picture is, the design, manner, and colour are clearly Holbeinesque.

A contemporary inscription—

'Ætati suæ. Ao. 1543'
· 30

—across the top of the panel shows that it was painted in the year that Wishart left Cambridge, and, as Holbein was in England and did not die until near the end of that year, it is possible that he painted it himself. At the same time, its condition makes any attribution uncertain, and 'painted in the style of Holbein' seems the most suitable description.

In 1631 Pitarrow was sold by the Wisharts to David, Lord Carnegie, and remained in the possession of his descendants for exactly two hundred years, when it was purchased by Mr. Crombie, advocate in Aberdeen. The old house, which had been pulled down a few years before the second transference, contained a number of mural paintings, including one supposed to be a satire on the Romish Church, and these were destroyed. Several pictures escaped that fate, and were sold. The late Archibald Wishart, W.S., a descendant of the Pitarrow family, purchased the portrait reproduced, and, a few years later, had it engraved by G. B. Shaw. In 1898 his widow, Mrs. May, bequeathed it to the Scottish National Portrait Gallery.

The only other portrait of any age, with pretensions to represent Wishart, is in the University of Glasgow, but it belongs to a series of made-up portraits, which were probably painted late in the following century.

22

PLATE VIII

CARDINAL DAVID BEATON

1494-1546

Painter : unknown.
Date : probably about 1541.
Size : 26¼ × 21½ ins.
Reproduced by permission of the present proprietor.

THE son of John Bethune of Balfour, for such is the old spelling of the name, he was nephew to the Archbishop of Glasgow and St. Andrews, and was early destined for the Church. After studying at St. Andrews and Glasgow he was sent to Paris to complete his education, and from 1519 to 1525 he represented Scotland at the French court. In 1528 the Archbishop had resigned the abbacy of Arbroath in his favour, and in 1537 he was given a French bishopric ; Pope Paul III. made him a Cardinal in 1538, and the following year he succeeded his uncle as Archbishop of St. Andrews. Previous to the last appointment, which made him Primate of the Scottish Church, he had exercised considerable influence in Scottish affairs, and had been employed frequently in foreign embassies. Now he was all for the French alliance, which at once strengthened his personal position and the Church to which he belonged, and, although for a short time after the death of James v. the English and Reformation party was in the ascendant, Beaton continued the most influential man in Scotland until his death. He specially distinguished himself by his zeal in religious persecution, and of all the clergy of the old faith he has left the most lasting impression on the popular imagination. In particular the martyrdom of George Wishart, the most eloquent of the Protestant preachers, whose death he witnessed from his castle walls, has left a stigma on his name, while it was the origin of a revenge that cost him his life. Two Leslies of Rothes, Kirkcaldy of Grange, and Melville of Raith were the principals in a plot to cut him off, and, seizing the castle of St. Andrews by stratagem early on the morning of the 29th May 1546, they despatched him in his own room. In answer to the demands of the citizens, who would not credit his death, his body was hung in a sheet from the window from which he had watched the burning of Wishart not three months before.

NO problem in Scottish portraiture is more puzzling than that of Cardinal Beaton. In many cases, where several types of portrait of one person exist, they can be reconciled: the two said to represent Beaton are irreconcilable, and the question as to which is to be accepted has to be faced. Pennant's *Tour in Scotland* (vol. iii.), Smith's *Iconographia*, and Lodge's big portrait book, all contain engravings of a picture in the Duke of Hamilton's apartments at Holyrood: a clean-shaven man of middle age, with long black hair covering his ears, very dark eyes under definitely marked eyebrows, a fairly long nose, rather full lips, and a well-formed but heavy chin; he wears a black callot or skull-cap with a red edging, a white linen falling collar of medium width with broad square ends, and a black tunic or robe; and the head and figure, seen to the waist, are half turned to the left. The type is clearly marked, and two portraits at Balfour, the old home of Beaton's family in Fifeshire, and a third in possession of another branch of the family—although the face in them is more intellectual, with less up-curved eyebrows, a more prominent nose, and a less heavy chin —may be said to confirm it. The set of the head, the lighting, the costume, and the general air of the pictures are almost identical. In the upper left corner of the pictures at Balfour, one of which is evidently copied from the other, an inscription reads 'David Betien cardinalis presbiter St. Step. de Monte Calio episcopus Meripoisensis de St. Andrew Archipiscopus,' and the same inscription occurs on the copy of this or a similar portrait, which was made by J. Nairne in 1844 and now hangs in the senate-room at St. Andrews. But in it the colour of robes and cap has been altered to a cardinal's scarlet. The costume of the Holyrood and Balfour portraits, however, is clearly that of the middle of the seventeenth century. It closely resembles that worn by divines and lawyers in England, while it is almost the same as that in portraits of Archbishop Sharp (1618-1679). Moreover, the style of painting belongs to that period. In the Bethune versions also a scarlet cap of biretta shape has been added at a later date—he wears two caps in these pictures—and as the inscription is probably of the same time, it seems as if these likenesses of some seventeenth-century personage had been converted into portraits of the Cardinal. The small respect in which they are held at Balfour still further discredits this type, which must

24

be regarded as impossible as a portrait of him. On the other hand, another portrait at Balfour has always been prized and considered an authentic rendering of David Beaton. As may be seen from the reproduction, it represents a quite different man from those just described. His hair, moustache, and chin tuft are a light sandy colour; his eyes are very dark blue-black; and his costume of scarlet cap, white collar, scarlet hood, and scarlet tippet, with buttons down the front, is exactly like that in authentic portraits of Cardinals Wolsey and Pole, his contemporaries in England. The sleek, crafty look is such as may well be associated with Beaton's known character. In the picture he seems, what Hill Burton describes him, 'more of a Frenchman and a servant of the Guises than of a Scotsman.' A portrait very similar to this, at Blairs, the Roman Catholic College near Aberdeen, is said to have come from the Scots College at Rome. It was engraved as frontispiece for the *Liber S. Thome de Aberbrothoc* (vol. ii.), edited by Cosmo Innes and Patrick Chalmers of Auldbar for the Ballantyne Club, and published in 1856. An inscription upon it refers to the Cardinal's death; but the picture is old and its origin interesting. The exact date when it was brought to Blairs is not known, but while still in Rome it was copied (*circa* 1820) by Giles, an Aberdeen artist. That copy is now at Fyvie Castle. Before I ascertained the history of the Blairs version, I had conjectured, from the age of the person represented and the appearance of the picture, that the Balfour portrait had been painted in Italy during Beaton's visit to Rome in 1541 with the intention of obtaining appointment as papal legate, and while still inclined to think the Blairs portrait more recent than that at Balfour, the history of the former goes a considerable way in confirming this hypothesis. Everything considered—the style of picture, the type of man, the costume, and the Bethune family tradition—there is the strongest likelihood that the Balfour portrait, here reproduced, is a true likeness of Cardinal Beaton.

PLATE IX

LORD DARNLEY AND HIS BROTHER

Painter: LUCAS DE HEERE (1534-1584).
Date: 1563.
Size: panel 25 × 15 ins.
In the possession of H.M. THE KING, by whose gracious permission
it is reproduced.   At Windsor Castle.

HENRY STUART, LORD DARNLEY
CONSORT OF MARY QUEEN OF SCOTS
1546-1567

ELDEST son of Matthew Stuart, Earl of Lenox, and his wife, Lady Margaret Douglas, daughter of Margaret, Queen of James IV., by her second husband, the Earl of Angus, Henry Stuart, Lord Darnley, was a second cousin of the Queen of Scots, and after her the nearest lineal heir to the throne of England, and it was to unite his claims to her own that Mary married him. With this intention she recalled his father and him from England, and found Darnley eager to fall in with her plan. They met at Wemyss Castle, in Fife, on 18th February 1565; a month later he was knighted and created Earl of Ross; on July 22 he was advanced to the dukedom of Albany; and a week later they were married at Holyrood. But before two months had passed Randolph wrote to Queen Elizabeth that he had shown himself unworthy and unfitted for the high place his marriage had given him; and his jealousy being aroused by Mary's partiality for her secretary, the Italian, Rizzio, he joined in a plot for his removal. After the murder he tried to save himself by betraying his confederates; but, his complicity being fully disclosed, he completely forfeited his wife's regard. The birth of a son, after-

26

LORD DARNLEY & HIS BROTHER.

wards James VI., made little difference in their relations, and he went to Glasgow with the intention of quitting Scotland, but, taking smallpox, could not. The Queen, now in Bothwell's toils, visited him, a reconciliation seemed to take place, and he accompanied her to Edinburgh; but a few days later, on the morning of 10th February 1567, his lodging at Kirk-o'-Field was blown up, and the King's dead body and that of his servant were found lying in an adjoining garden. Bothwell was prime mover in this murder, but it is all but certain that Mary was directly accessory.

According to Pitscottie, Darnley 'appeared verrie pleasant in the sight of gentlewomen,' and Mary, at one time, thought him 'the best proportioned long man she had seen.' But his good looks were all that were in his favour. Of despicable and weak character, he was vain and vicious, inconsiderate and over-bearing.

CHARLES STUART, EARL OF LENOX

1557–1577

CHARLES, the second son of the Earl and Countess of Lenox, who survived infancy, succeeded his father in 1571; married in 1574 Elizabeth, daughter of Sir William Cavendish and his wife, the celebrated Bess of Harwick; and died in 1577. His only child was Lady Arabella Stuart (1575-1615), whose proximity to the throne was a cause of constant trouble to herself, and ended in her dying a prisoner in the Tower.

'The Lord Darnley and his brother at length in little sold to Mr. Murray as appraised 28 Octr. 1651, for £6,' when the collection of King Charles I. was dispersed by the Commonwealth, is now in H.M. the King's collection at Windsor Castle. De Heere's monogram is on the cross-rail of the table behind, the date 1568 at the feet of, the brothers, and this inscription runs across the top and bottom of the picture: 'Thes be the sones of the Right Honerables Therlle of Lenoxe and the Lady Margaret-Grace, Countes of Lenox and Angwyse. Henry Stewarde, Lord Darnley and Dowglas, ætatis 17. Chariles Stewarde, his brother, ætatis 6.' The monogram and date are contemporary, and, probably, the inscription; the lettering has the character of the period, and Darnley's family was fond of inscriptions, as the memorial picture and the elaborate

SCOTTISH PORTRAITS

'Darnley' jewel in the Royal collection show. He and his parents were in London in 1563, and he left for Scotland in the spring of 1565. A considerably larger but—excepting the background, which is a simple brown-panelled wall, the placing of the inscriptions, and the date, which is given as 1562 —similar picture hangs in Holyrood. That reproduced is the better, however, and almost certainly the original. Both were at one time at Hampton Court. From them we learn that Darnley's hair was warm brown, and his eyes hazel (yellow and blue), and that his brother's hair was rather lighter and his eyes bluer. Both are dressed in black, but while Darnley has white ruffles in both pictures, those worn by Charles are dark in the smaller, and white edged with black in the larger. They are probably the most interesting and authentic portraits of Darnley, and show very clearly that long-legged, short-waisted appearance which was subject for remark amongst his contemporaries. It is known that James VI. had his father's remains re-interred in Westminster, and Lord Hailes tells how, in his day, Darnley's thigh-bone was shown for money there, and that a philosopher calculated that he must have been eight feet in height.

Of other authentic portraits of Darnley that in the possession of Lord Bolton, representing him at the age of nine (c. 1554), is the most interesting. The panel (36 × 30 ins.) is branded with Charles I.'s mark, and, although unmentioned in Vanderdoort's catalogue, probably belonged to him. '31 May 1639. Given to my Sovereign Lord the King by his Grace the Duke of Lennox,' is written on a paper stuck to the back. In it he has warm fair hair and eyebrows, and grey eyes, is dressed in black, and wears a black cap with a white feather: the face is cubbier and the expression pleasanter than in the portrait reproduced. It is signed with an initial not unlike De Heere's. A second picture in the same collection also bears Charles I.'s brand, and, like the other, it is supposed to have come to its present owners through a daughter of the Duke of Monmouth.

PLATE X

KING JAMES VI. AT HIS FATHER'S TOMB

'THE DARNLEY MEMORIAL PICTURE'

Painter: LEVINUS VOGELNARIUS (?).
Date: 1567-8.
Size: 89 × 57 ins.
In the possession of H.M. THE KING, by whose gracious permission
it is reproduced. At Holyrood.

AFTER Darnley's murder (10th February 1567), the Earl of Lenox, the dead King's father, sought by every means in his power to have the guilty parties brought to trial, but the Queen's infatuation for Bothwell, and her probable connivance, if not her actual co-operation, in the deed, combined with the rank of some of Bothwell's associates, resulted in an assize (12th April), which was in reality a fiasco. Balked of direct and immediate vengeance, Lenox retired to England, and the picture reproduced was probably in part a result of this visit. It is at all events convincing evidence of the feelings of the Lenox family in connection with the murder, and of the desire of the Earl and Countess to impress the young King, their grandson, with a sense of what his father had suffered at the hands of Bothwell and the Queen.

Although painted for the express purpose of remaining with the King as a constant reminder of his father's murder, the picture did not pass into the Royal collection until much later. It does not figure in the catalogue of his pictures or in those of Charles II.'s or James II.'s collections, and it was in the possession of the last Duke of Richmond and Lenox at Cobham Hall, Kent, at his death in 1672. It then became the property of his only sister, Lady Catherine O'Brien, from whom the present Earls of Darnley are descended, but passed to the widow of that lady's only son, who married as her second husband Lord Dempster,

29

afterwards Earl of Pomfret. Their son, the Earl of Pomfret, presented it to George II. in 1738, since when it has remained in the Royal collection, since 1900 at Holyrood.

Another version, almost identical in size, was discovered in the Duke of Richmond, Lenox, and Aubigny's Castle of Aubigny in France (the 2nd Duke of Richmond of this creation succeeded the Duchess of Portsmouth in the dukedom of Aubigny in 1734) before 1742, when George Vertue (1684-1756) made an engraving from them—he worked from both—and wrote an elaborate description founded in part upon that compiled by James Anderson, a Scottish antiquary, for the Earl of Oxford in 1727. The French version, which is supposed to have been sent by Earl Matthew to his brother John, Lord Aubigny, was in a very dilapidated state, but, by comparison with Lord Pomfret's, it was 'perfected,' the other being retouched in parts also. It is now at Goodwood. Except in minor details, these pictures resemble each other closely, but that at Holyrood is undoubtedly the original, and in addition it has been much less repainted. Vertue found a signature upon the Pomfret picture, but was unable to say whether it was Levinus Venetianus or Vogelarius. He inclined to the former and put it on his engraving, but careful examination makes one think the latter, with the spelling 'Vogelnarius,' more probable. Neither artist is known, and no name resembling either is to be found in the lists of aliens working in England at this period. Walpole, who does not seem to have noticed that it was painted in London, says that Vertue thought it might be by 'Lovino,' a nephew of Pordenone, by whom Charles I. had a picture. This is improbable, however, the work bearing little trace of Italian influence, and considerable resemblance to Netherlandish art. Lucas de Heere has also been suggested, and that attribution has some support in the fact that he did paint and sign the group of Darnley and his brother, but neither the style of this particular work nor the blurred signature warrants the supposition.

Vertue's engraving gives little idea of the strength of portraiture in the original, and presents several variations from it, of which the more notable are the insertion of a helmet between Darnley's knees and feet and the inscription upon the edge of the cenotaph. But for these he had warrant in the Goodwood version. In the separate plate of the 'Battle Array,' which he made about the same time, the variations are of little importance.

In a chapel which contains an effigy of Darnley upon an elaborate sarcophagus, King James VI., his son, his parents, the Earl and Countess of Lenox,

80

KING JAMES VI. AT HIS FATHER'S TOMB

and his brother, Charles, are represented kneeling before an altar, upon which stands a coloured image of our Lord, beseeching God to avenge the murder. The separate petitions are printed in Latin upon scrolls or ribbons over the heads of the respective petitioners; but that of the Earl and his lady being a united one a single scroll encircles their heads. Immediately over the effigy are the Royal Standard of Scotland and the Scottish Ensign with the St. Andrew's Cross surmounted of an open crown (the field of the latter is Gules and not Azure, as it should be), and above the Earl and Countess is a third flag with Darnley's paternal and feudal quarterings. The effigy represents him in gilded armour, and the head, hands, and ruffles are coloured realistically. Upon the side of the marble tomb are three shields ensigned with closed crowns and surrounded by the collars of different orders. In the centre are the Scottish Arms and the Collar of the Thistle; to the left the first and fourth quarters of the flag on the right are impaled with the Scottish Lion within the Royal tressure, and the shield is encircled by the Collar and Badge of the Order of St. Michel; to the right the second and third quarters of the same flag again impale Scotland, and are surrounded by the insignia of the French order. On each side of the centre shield a medallion depicts a scene from the murder; at the corners are angel figures; modelled cherub heads are inserted in the spaces between, and the architecture is further enriched by gilt mouldings. The heraldry is coloured and the modelled decoration is gilded, the gilding being represented by pigment.

In the upper left corner, near the circular window, an inscription gives, like a modern headline, the gist of the picture. It reads, 'The tragical and lamentable murder of the most serene Henry King of Scots,' and a long inscription, in black letters on a white ground, directly below the same window, sets forth the complicacy of the Queen and Bothwell in the murder, and gives the ages of the persons represented when the picture was in progress. The young King was sixteen months; the Earl and Countess, respectively fifty and fifty-one; Charles Stuart, eleven. The passage referring to the Queen's connection with the tragedy is blurred in the Royal picture. It had been completely obliterated at some time, and was repainted from the Goodwood version. In the centre, just over the effigy, a painted board bears an heroic poem extolling the dead man's virtues, gifts, and graces in most extravagant terms, and towards the right a similar board tells the *raison d'être* of the picture.

In the lower left corner is a small picture of the 'Battle Array at

81

Carberry,' where Queen Mary, forced to part from Bothwell, surrendered to the Confederate Lords. The left foreground is occupied by a suggestion of Edinburgh with Salisbury Crags and Arthur's Seat, and beyond a bare green landscape stretches to a distance of blue-green hills. Towards the left the Confederate army is drawn up in three divisions. Over the centre fly seven flags—beginning at the left—with the arms of Graham, Earl of Montrose; Elphinstone; Lord Lindsay of the Byres; Ruthven; Erskine, Earl of Mar; Stuart, Earl of Athole; and Cunninghame, Earl of Glencairn, and before it is borne a banner with the motto, 'Judge and revenge my cause, O Lord,' and the device of the infant prince kneeling beside his dead father, which seem repeated on the flag of the farther wing, which consists of cavalry. Over the right and nearer division are three flags, that of the Earl of Morton, to the right, and two others on which the blazoning is indefinite in the picture, although in Vertue's print they are shown as Hume in the centre, and Moray (as Mar) to the left. In this connection it is worth while recalling that Buchanan names the Earls of Glencairn, Athole, and Mar as leaders of the centre; and Morton and Hume of the right. Over a dense clump of spearmen, posted on a knoll to the right, floats the Royal Standard of Scotland, and on its left front are four (?) Scottish ensigns. This is the Queen's and Bothwell's force. Just in front of it a woman in a red habit, the Queen, and several armed and mounted men, one of whom is probably Bothwell, are gathered, while cannon fire a salute amid a blare of trumpets. Farther down, and approaching the opposing force, the Queen, led by a man on foot (Kirkcaldy of Grange?), and accompanied by another lady, Mary Seton, on horseback, is shown again, while to the right of the knoll, two horsemen, with ' Boithuille's departing' written above them, are galloping off. The latter are repeated more than once in the distance. A castle in the middle distance on the left may be intended for Dunbar, and, although unnamed in the picture, it is so labelled in Vertue's engraving. This subsidiary picture is surrounded by a brown-painted frame, with a long inscription dealing with the surrender. Like all the other inscriptions, except those in the Carberry, it is in Latin.

A most interesting commentary on the 'Battle Array' exists in the Record Office. It is a 'Drawing in colours, representing the meeting of the Lords with the Queen of Scotland in the field' (22 × 14 ins.), and is said to be contemporary. In it, however, the right wing of the Confederates is alone seen, and it is broken into three separate troops, designated as those of Lords

82

KING JAMES VI. AT HIS FATHER'S TOMB

Morton and Hume, and Kirkcaldy of Grange. As in the picture, the Queen's army is posted on a knoll to the right, and she, with the same attendants, is approaching the Confederate Lords. The topography of the drawing is more correct than that of the picture.

Painted, as we learn from one of the many inscriptions, for the Earl and Countess of Lenox, because they were growing old, to remind the King, their grandson, of the atrocious murder of his father until such time as he should be revenged upon the murderers, this curious picture forms a document of some historical importance and contains several portraits of considerable interest. As the King's age is given as sixteen months, it must have been begun by October 1567, that is within eight months of the murder and only four after Mary's surrender at Carberry, and it was completed in London in January 1568, some four months later. It is thus a contemporary production, and, although obviously painted for a special purpose, a notable piece of evidence. In the main it corroborates the usual view, and in the inset of Carberry lays special stress upon several points which have appealed to popular feeling. In the picture itself the most interesting divergence from accepted theories is found in one of the medallions on the cenotaph. The fact that the bodies of Darnley and his servant bore no marks of the explosion, but had marks of other violence, has usually been considered conclusive that they attempted to escape but were discovered and strangled. This medallion, however, suggests, not only by inference but in words, a variation on that explanation. While the medallion to the right shows them lying in the garden and has an inscription to that effect, the other and its inscription deal with the 'Murder of the said King and his servant in their beds.' For these medallions the Goodwood picture is the authority. They were obliterated and repainted on the other.

The portraits are verified, of course, by the conditions under which the picture was painted, and, despite some repainting in faces and hands, those of the Earl and Countess and their younger son remain admirable likenesses. That of the infant King must necessarily have been painted without reference to life, and the head is that of a child of four or five, the hands those of a grown man. And here a difference between the two versions may be mentioned. While in the Holyrood picture he wears a whitish-grey and ermine cloak, and kneels on a grey mat before a grey cushion on a grey desk, these articles are dark purple-green in that at Goodwood. Darnley's face was probably founded upon an existing portrait, but it is more sharply cut in type, due in part perhaps to repainting, than the De Heere rendering or the kneeling figure on his mother's tomb. Of no woman of the period is there clearer and less contradictory artistic record than of Margaret Douglas. The admirable effigy in Westminster Abbey and a number of authentic portraits all agree in representing her much as she is in this picture. Of her husband, on the other hand, this is the only reliable portrait, but internal evidence, combined with the veracity of those of his Countess and his son—the latter may be compared with one or two authentic portraits—gives it every claim to credence. Here one may note that he is of pale complexion, has light brown hair, beard, and moustache, and blue-grey eyes under very slightly marked eyebrows.

Mr. W. Rae Macdonald, Carrick Pursuivant, very kindly went over the heraldry in the picture for me, and, as I have been unable to incorporate his careful analysis in detail, my obligation to him is greater than is evident.

PLATE XI

LORD JAMES STUART
EARL OF MORAY

1531 ?–1570

Painter and date : unknown.
Size : panel 14½ × 10½ ins.
In the possession of the Trustees of the DUKE OF HAMILTON.   At Holyrood.

LORD JAMES STUART, natural son of James v., King of Scotland, and Lady Margaret Erskine, daughter of the 5th Earl of Mar, was only about seven years old when he was made Prior of St. Andrews. He studied at St. Andrews, and in 1548 accompanied his half-sister, the young Queen, to France, which he frequently revisited; but from early in his career he sympathised with the Reformation, and in 1557 he was one of those who signed a letter asking Knox to return to Scotland. Renouncing the Church, he soon became the leader of the Lords of the Congregation and the dominant political personality in Scotland, and when, on the death of Francis ii., Mary returned to Scotland (1561), she found him her wisest councillor. But opposition to her marriage with Darnley cost him place and power, and, though after the murder of Rizzio they seemed reconciled, the Queen never forgave him. He was in St. Andrews when Darnley was removed, and before Bothwell and Mary married he had gone to France, where he remained until the Queen signed her abdication and nominated him Regent. His work in tranquillising Scotland and settling the affairs of the Church was soon interrupted by Mary's escape from Lochleven, but he dealt with the crisis promptly, and her army being defeated at Langside, she fled to England. There her whole conduct came under review, and Moray, in the interests of his country, as well as in vindication of his own actions, reluctantly consented to become her chief accuser. Yet he was engaged in negotiations with Elizabeth for her deliverance

85

and residence in Scotland, when he was assassinated by James Hamilton of Bothwellhaugh in the streets of Linlithgow.

In Scottish history Moray is known as the 'Good Regent,' and he deserves the name. If he had a knack of looking through his fingers at questionable deeds in which he did not care to take an active part, he stands out clearly from his compeers as a statesman of large views and noble purposes. Personal ambition he was not free from, but, as it happened, his personal ends coincided with the general good, and on several occasions he chose the course which seemed opposed to his own advancement. His administration of affairs was stern but just, his interest in Protestantism was sincere, and after Mary and Knox he is the most commanding figure of his time.

WHILE this portrait has little but tradition to support it, and its being in the possession of the house of Hamilton, the Regent's inveterate enemies, is not in its favour, it is the only portrait of him now existing which has claims to consideration, and it is not contradicted by any contemporary description. Moreover, several portraits at Holyrood, now belonging to the Hamiltons, would seem to have passed into their hands through their hereditary keepership of the Palace. The fine portrait of Queen Elizabeth, said to have been sent to Queen Mary as a birthday gift, is a case in point, and this portrait may owe its present location to a like cause. There was at one time at Donibristle, the Fifeshire seat of the Earls of Moray, a portrait supposed to be that of the Regent, but it perished in the last burning of that fated house, and all that remains to indicate its character is a poor stipple engraving, of which a copy is preserved in the Scottish National Portrait Gallery. It is not much to go by, but, while obviously a different rendering, it may well represent the same man as the Holyrood picture. A contemporary painting on panel, the latter, although considerably rubbed and retouched, is an admirable piece of portraiture by a French or Flemish painter, and represents a man of between thirty and forty, with a short, full beard, moustache and hair of dark warm brown, keen medium brown eyes, and alert and intelligent expression. He wears a close-fitting black doublet, with a high collar finishing in a small, white ruff, a costume such as one finds in the portraits of Charles IX. of France (1550-1574) and his courtiers.

86

IOANNES CNOXVS.

PLATE XII

JOHN KNOX

1505–1572

Wood-engraving, by an unknown artist, after ADRIANC VAENSOUN.
Date of painting, 1579; of engraving, 1580.
Reproduced full size.

BORN at Giffordgate, Haddington, to burgess parents, John Knox was educated at Glasgow University, where for a short time he studied under John Major. He took minor orders and seems to have practised as a notary in his native district, but conversion to the reformed doctrines made the Church an impossible career, and he became a tutor in a Protestant family. Being present in the castle of St. Andrews when it capitulated, after the doing to death of Cardinal Beaton, he was carried captive to France, and for nineteen months rowed in the galleys. He then found asylum in England and, later, in Geneva, where he associated with Calvin. In 1555 he returned to Scotland, and, joining the Lords of the Congregation, exercised a commanding influence on the course of the Reformation in his own country; but less than a year later he again retired to Geneva. Back in Scotland once more in 1559, he became a still greater power among his countrymen: the Confession of Faith was adopted, and he was ordained minister of St. Giles, Edinburgh. It was about this time that his famous interviews with his Queen, Mary Stuart, took place. Like many of the Scots lords, he had to retire to England after the murder of Rizzio, but events subsequent to the murder of Darnley enabled him to return, and he continued to exercise unabated power until his death, by which time the Protestant cause had triumphed definitely. Over his grave the Regent Morton pronounced the memorable words, 'Here lies one who neither flattered nor feared any flesh.'

With nothing of romance about him; with few of those charms of presence or manner which win willing admiration; perfervid, unforgiving, and somewhat forbidding—John Knox is yet the most potent personality in his country's history.

87

SCOTTISH PORTRAITS

He was not the first to preach the doctrines of the Reformation in Scotland; Lollards had been martyred in Kyle before he was born, and as a youth he had carried a sword before Maister George Wishart in that preaching crusade in the Lothians which ended in the fiery pile at St. Andrews; but his was the genius and the power which gave Protestantism its democratic basis and its strong foothold in Scotland. The story of this struggle and triumph is most graphically told by himself in his *History of the Reformation in Scotland*, published a year after his death.

AN entry in the Lord High Treasurer's accounts for June 1581, to the effect that payment had been made to 'Adrianc Vaensoun, Fleming painter, for two pictures painted be him, and send to Theodorus Besa,' had been held to verify the wood-engraving of Knox which appeared in Beza's *Icones* (published at Geneva in 1580), and was repeated in line-engraving by Hondius for Verheiden's *Images* (1602), until, in *Fraser's Magazine* for April 1875, Thomas Carlyle refused to accept it, and brought forward what is now known as the 'Somerville' portrait to take its place. He wrote a good deal against the Beza and much more in favour of his prodigy, but the former was not convincing, and the latter may be fairly summed up by saying that it was Knox because it looked like what Carlyle thought Knox must have looked. James Drummond, R.S.A., who possessed great knowledge of both archæology and art, replied in terms which completely shattered the claims of Carlyle's fancy and went far to establish the reliability of Beza's print. But it remained for Professor Hume Brown, the biographer of Knox, to place the latter beyond dispute. Twenty years later a letter was placed in his hands which at once verifies the portrait and gives a striking verbal picture of the Reformer. Written by Sir Peter Young (1544-1628) from Edinburgh on 13th November 1579, and addressed to Beza, it deals with other matters, but the paragraphs relevant are as follows :—

'With regard to your request that I should send you the portraits of the illustrious men who have toiled for the glory of God among us, and specially that of Mr. Knox, set it for ever down to the negligence (not to use a stronger word) of our nation that it has never given heed to this duty. Not even of Knox, a man worthy of eternal memory, does any representation exist. However, I have approached certain of our artists, and if they stand by their promises, you will receive a portrait of him along with this letter. Meanwhile, with my own pencil I will describe his face and bearing from my recollection of him, and from the report of those who were most intimate with him while he yet lived. The whole story of his life you will hear from Mr. Lowson. In stature, then, he was slightly under the middle height, of well-knit and graceful figure, with shoulders somewhat broad, longish fingers, head of moderate size, hair black, complexion somewhat dark, and a general appearance not unpleasing. In his stern and severe countenance there was a natural dignity and majesty not without a certain grace, and in anger there was an air of command on his brow. Under a somewhat narrow forehead his brows stood out in a slight ridge over his ruddy and slightly swelling cheeks, so that his eye seemed to retreat into his head. The colour of his eyes was bluish-grey; their glance keen and animated. His face was rather long; his nose of more than ordinary length; the mouth large; the lips full, the upper a little thicker than the lower; his beard black mingled with grey, very long and moderately thick.

'Just as I am signing this letter, an artist has opportunely come in, and brought in one box the likenesses of Knox and Buchanan.'

Thus it is proved that the portrait engraved for Beza was painted in 1579, published in 1580, and paid for in 1581. Few historical portraits are better authenticated. No Flemish painter, as he is clearly stated to have been, of the name is to be found in any of the dictionaries, and no other portrait by him is known, yet it was the fortune of this otherwise unknown artist to preserve for posterity the likeness of one of the greatest of men. He may be the same as the 'Hadrian Vauson paynter to His Majesty,' who in 1594 became security, along with the Ambassador for the Lords of the Confederate Provinces, for a Flemish skipper, as recorded in the Register of the Privy Council; but, even were that certain, we would be no wiser, for nothing is known of that Court painter. No other authentic portrait of Knox exists.

PLATE XIII

SIR WILLIAM KIRKCALDY
OF GRANGE

Executed 1573

Painter: François Clouet (1518?-1573?)
Date: *circa* 1555.
Size: panel 12 × 8¾ ins.
In the possession of the Hon. Mrs. Baillie Hamilton.

ELDEST son of Sir James Kirkcaldy, Lord High Treasurer, he was brought up as an opponent of French influence in Scotland, and was present at the murder of Cardinal Beaton, after which he was for some time a prisoner in France. Escaping to England he returned to France to serve with distinction as an officer of light horse, and became a favourite with Henri II. In 1557, however, he was back in Scotland, where he took part in negotiations with England, and acted with the Lords of the Congregation in opposition to the Queen-Mother. When Queen Mary returned to her own country (1561), he rendered her important service and was formally restored to his estates, but, opposing the Darnley marriage, he was put to the horn. After Rizzio's murder he was received into favour again, but when Mary married Bothwell he joined the Confederate Lords, and was present with them at Carberry Hill, where she chose him to receive her surrender. Moray appointed him Governor of Edinburgh Castle, and he contributed greatly to the victory over Mary's forces at Langside; but after the Regent's death he went over to the Queen's party and held the castle in her name. There he was joined by Maitland of Lethington. They were closely besieged by Morton, who, however, would have spared them if Kirkcaldy would have consented to the ruin of the Hamiltons; and after a gallant resistance they surrendered the castle to the Scottish troops and themselves to the English commander. Transferred to Morton's keeping, their fate was sealed, and on 3rd August 1573 Kirkcaldy was executed at the Cross.

40

SIR WILLIAM KIRKCALDY OF GRANGE
Executed 1573

SIR WILLIAM KIRKCALDY OF GRANGE

A PASSAGE in Sir James Melville's *Memoirs* describes Kirkcaldy as 'humble, gentle, and meek, like a lamb in the house and like a lion in the field, a lusty, stark, and well-proportioned personage, hardy, and of magnanimous courage,' but the words convey little impression of his personal appearance, which, so far as I know, is only pictured once and that in a portrait which has little more than tradition and internal evidence to support it. It is so interesting, however, and accords so well with what is known of Kirkcaldy, that it is included here. Acquired by the Breadalbane family from the celebrated collection of Quintin Crawford of Paris, it is said to have been painted while Kirkcaldy was serving as a cavalry officer in France, 1558-7. It is painted on panel, and, although retouched in parts, may be described as an excellent example of French painting of the period, possibly by François Clouet, to whom it is attributed. He has yellow fair hair, moustache, and eyebrows, and a slight growth of the same colour on the chin; his eyes are grey mixed with hazel; his complexion is pale, and his thin and colourless lips are pretty close-shut. The costume consists of a sleeveless red tunic, with narrow yellow embroidery and gold buttons, over a bright green undergarment, and he wears a black hat, with white feather plume and little buckles, of which five are seen, and a small piped white ruff. Plain grey-green background.

PLATE XIV

WILLIAM MAITLAND
OF LETHINGTON

1528 ?–1573

Painter and date unknown.
Size: 27 × 22½ ins.
In the possession of the EARL OF LAUDERDALE.

'SECRETARY LETHINGTON,' as he was called, was the eldest son of Sir Richard Maitland, who made a famous collection of Scots poems, and, educated at St. Andrews and abroad, he was scholar and phrase-maker as well as diplomatist. He commenced his official career in the service of Mary of Guise, the Queen-Regent, but in 1559, being convinced of the advantage of an English over a French alliance, went over to the opposition party, in which he soon took a prominent place. On the return of the young Queen, he was chosen Secretary; and, being intrusted with the management of her relations with England, tried to reconcile his mistress and Elizabeth. He was also deeply engaged in negotiations for Mary's marriage, and, the Spanish suit having failed, he supported Darnley's claims. But connection with Rizzio's murder led to disgrace. His services were too valuable, however, to be dispensed with, and soon afterwards he was in favour again and married to Mary Fleming, one of the Queen's ladies. He was concerned in ridding the Queen of Darnley and accompanied her to Seton after the murder, and, while disapproving of her marrying Bothwell, he did not oppose it. But he tried to save her from the consequences of that rash act, and, without breaking with the Regent Moray, he worked for her restoration. After the Regent's death he became head of the Queen's party in Scotland and joined Kirkcaldy of Grange in Edinburgh Castle. Two months later they surrendered to Drury, the English commander, but that availed them nothing. Kirkcaldy was executed, and Maitland, who was far gone already, only escaped the same fate by dying in prison, it was said, by poison taken by himself.

42

SIR WILLIAM RUSSELL, LATER LORD RUSSELL
OF THORNHAUGH

WILLIAM MAITLAND OF LETHINGTON

A PORTRAIT of the Secretary is preserved at Thirlestane Castle, the Berwickshire seat of his family. It is by an unknown painter, probably of the Flemish school, and is marked in the upper left corner 'Secretary Leithington.' The face, seen half turned to the right, is long and very peaked towards the chin. He has a long nose, straight and thin bridged; medium brown eyes; warm light-brown beard and moustache (beneath which bright red lips show somewhat prominently), and hair of darker brown. His black velvet cap has a beaded band, and his black coat has two gold shoulder straps and is trimmed with broad stripes of brown fur down the front. There is a strong resemblance between this portrait and those of his brother John, first Lord Thirlestane and Chancellor of Scotland (1545?-1595). The general type of the head and the colour and cut of beard and moustache are very similar; but the eyes of the Chancellor are darker, his nose thinner and more curved, and while the brows of both are pretty straight, those of the Secretary are more arched and higher over the eyes. Other minor differences prove that the likeness, so striking at first sight, is only a family resemblance. The engravings in Pinkerton, in which both figure, are too poor to enable the comparison to be made there; but if the Secretary in this series is compared with the Lord Thirlestane in Sir John Skelton's *Mary Stuart*—where by some mischance it is given as Maitland of Lethington—the difference will be apparent. One is not so certain, however, whether this particular portrait of the Secretary is an original or a later copy of an original now lost. The corresponding portrait of his brother seems a copy of another portrait at Thirlestane, dated 1589.

PLATE XV

JAMES, 2ND EARL OF ARRAN

Died 1575

Painter: CORNELIUS KETEL (1548-1609).
Date: 1573-5.
Size: panel 45½ × 42½ ins.
In the possession of the Trustees of the DUKE OF HAMILTON.

JAMES HAMILTON was the eldest son of the 1st Earl of Arran, and grandson of James, 1st Lord Hamilton, and his wife the Princess Mary, daughter of King James II. He succeeded his father in 1529, and after Solway Moss and the death of James V. (1542) he was elected Regent of Scotland. Indolent and without special talent, he owed his position to his relationship to the Royal house, and his policy, being dictated by his own interests, gave satisfaction to none. At length the Queen-Mother virtually superseded him, and arranged to send her daughter, the little Queen Mary, to France. Although this blighted the hopes of Arran, who had designed marrying his eldest son to her, he consented, and was given the French duchy of Châtelherault (1549). Five years later he resigned the Regency, and when (1559) Edinburgh fell into the hands of the Protestant lords, he withdrew his support from the Queen-Regent, but tried to maintain a neutral position. He was well received by Queen Mary when she returned from France, but her marriage with Darnley upset his plans, and he went to France. In 1569 he came back to Scotland, where he supported the party of the Queen, now in prison in England, until 1573. Two years later he died at Hamilton. He had changed his party whenever his personal ends could be served; he had been Catholic and Protestant by turns, and alternately in favour of a French or an English alliance.

IN this, his most authentic portrait, the Regent Arran looks, what he was, a shuffler. His look is furtive, his attitude apologetic and indeterminate, as if he was in difficulty how to stand to the artist. His eyebrows, moustache, and

44

JAMES 2ND EARL OF ARRAN
(1516-1575)

beard are white, his hair grey, his eyes dark grey; his cap and dress, edged with brown fur, are black, and he wears the collar and jewel of St. Michel. Upon the paper, painted in the upper right corner, is the inscription, 'Ætatis suæ 56. Ao. 1575'; and his armorial bearings, to the left, are encircled by the insignia of the French order. A portrait resembling that reproduced closely, but showing only the bust, is engraved in Pinkerton's *Scottish Gallery* : it was at that time in the possession of the Marquis of Abercorn, at Bentley Lodge, Harrow.

There is at Biel a picture (86 × 27 ins.) which has been exhibited as representing this noble, but the modern inscription, 'Duke of Chattelherault,' is contradicted by three heraldic shields with the names of Derrick Anthony and his two wives. It is dated 1568, and attributed to Zucchero.

As Ketel came to England in 1578, the portrait reproduced represents Arran towards the close of his life.

PLATE XVI

JAMES DOUGLAS, 4TH EARL OF MORTON

1530–1581

Painter: unknown.
Date: about 1577.
Size: panel 42 × 32 ins.
In the possession of the EARL OF MORTON.

SECOND son of Sir George Douglas of Pittendreich, who had been twice forfeited for treason, his education was neglected and his early years misspent, but great natural ability enabled him to attain great influence and prominence in the affairs of his country. In virtue of his wife he succeeded his father-in-law in the Morton title and estates (1553), and, favouring the cause of the Reformation, he was one of the original Lords of the Congregation. He was sworn a Privy Councillor in 1561, and two years later became Lord Chancellor, but, being engaged in the Rizzio conspiracy, had to fly the country (1567). Thinking to use him in his plans against Darnley, Bothwell secured his recall, but he would take no active part in the murder, and he was one of the most energetic of the Confederates to whom Mary surrendered at Carberry. The celebrated and much-discussed casket letters, which implicated Mary in the murder of her husband, fell into his hands, and he acted with Moray at Langside when the Queen's fate was sealed by the defeat of her army. In October 1572 he succeeded Mar as Regent, being the fourth within five years, and for five years he ruled Scotland with marked success, crushing the last hopes of the Queen's party by his treatment of Kirkcaldy and Maitland. Even after he demitted office he exercised great influence, but in 1581 the young King, acting on the advice of Morton's enemies, had him brought to trial as accessory to the death of his father Darnley. In such circumstances the result was certain, and Morton was executed by 'The Maiden,' a prototype of the guillotine introduced by himself.

46

JAMES DE TOBIAS 6TH EARL OF MORTON
REGENT OF SCOTLAND

JAMES DOUGLAS, 4TH EARL OF MORTON

SEVERAL good portraits of Morton exist, but all are versions of that at Dalmahoy, the seat of the Earls of Morton, near Edinburgh. A contemporary work, and always in the possession of the Morton family, it has never been challenged, and although Sir Herbert Maxwell, in his Douglas book, has brought forward, with considerable plausibility, a very interesting drawing in the possession of Sir T. Gibson Carmichael as probably a preliminary sketch for it, I am inclined to regard it as having been done from the picture at a much later date. The style of the drawing is not that of the period, the pencilling is too fresh and unrubbed to have stood three hundred and fifty years, and the profile sketch on the margin, which in the lithograph adds so much to its apparent claims, is far less spontaneous and veracious in the drawing itself. While none of the other versions is so complete as the Dalmahoy portrait, that at Newbattle, also on panel (44¼ × 30¼ ins.)—with differences in the background, the curtain is brown and not green, and the peep of landscape is omitted—is an excellent portrait of the man, and follows the other closely in the coloration of face and figure. Versions at Hamilton Palace (23 × 16¼) and the Binns (21½ × 18 ins.) show the bust only, but the latter has an inscription, 'Regent Morton, 1577, *Nec temere, nec timide,*' of considerable interest, as the date, falling in, as it does, with the apparent age of the man, supplies a likely date for the three-quarter length also. He was then forty-seven, and in his bushy red beard and moustache there is no hint of grey; his very small dark grey eyes are under darker brown eyebrows; his carriage is erect and alert; his left hand rests on his sword-hilt, his right on his waist. His costume and tall hat are black, the piped ruffles at neck and wrists are white, and yellow gloves lie on the red-covered table to the left. The green curtain in the background hangs in many folds and is looped up on the right, giving a peep of landscape with a castle, which has not, however, been recognised as one of several built by the Regent.

PLATE XVII

JAMES CRICHTON

1506–1582

Painter and date unknown.
Size: 29½ × 24½ ins.
In the possession of the Trustees of COLONEL GRAHAM of Airth.

TO many who use it, the descriptive epithet 'An Admirable Crichton' has no meaning beyond the implication of versatility. Yet it had a definite origin and was first applied to a particular person. James Crichton, who earned it, and whose exploits gave it currency and significance, was a young Scot of the sixteenth century, who had in his day a European reputation. Younger son of Robert Crichton of Cluny, he graduated at St. Andrews when fourteen, and soon afterwards set out on his travels. A remarkable swordsman and a past-master in all knightly graces, it was the combination of these with wonderful intellectual gifts which brought him fame and made his name the synonym for all-round accomplishment. His brilliant scholastic display before the doctors of the Paris Sorbonne illustrates one phase of his meteoric career, his triumphant encounters with several notorious duellists at Mantua another, while his friendship with learned men like Aldus, the printer, and his conquests amongst the fair sex were equally conspicuous. This paragon was treacherously slain by the son of the Duke of Mantua, to whom he had rendered great services, in or about 1582. If that date be correct, he was only twenty-two. It is more probable, however, that he lived some three years longer.

CRICHTON is represented in portraiture by two principal pictures and many copies. That, which passed into the possession of the Morisons of Bognie from the Crichtons of Frendraught, by marriage some two hundred years ago, has the better history, the tradition being that it was sent from Italy shortly before his death; but as it has been admirably engraved (see *Proceedings of Society of Antiquaries of Scotland*, vol. ii. part 2), while that at Airth, which is the

48

source of most copies, is only indifferently seen in Pennant's *Tour*, and there from a copy, the latter has been chosen for this series. It came into the possession of the Grahams through Lady Elizabeth Livingstone (sister of the last Earl of Callender, who was forfeited after the '15), that lady having married into the Airth family. The long inscription on the background is a quotation from John Johnston, and the lines first appeared in his *Heroes ex omni Historia Scotica lectissimi*, published in 1608. There the date of Crichton's death is given as 1581. These lines appear on the Bognie portrait also. In the portrait reproduced he has dark brown hair and dark grey eyes, wears a black doublet and a blue-white ruff, and, seated in a chair, holds in his right hand a sword and in his left a book. A notice of Crichton, printed at Venice in 1580, records that his face was marred by a birth-mark or mole about the right eye. This red-rose, as Manutius calls it, appears in most of the pictures. The Bognie portrait shows him without the emblematic accessories of sword and book, and while the face is rather more refined than in the Airth rendering, it has scarcely so much character. An engraving, showing the bust only and with the head turned in the opposite direction to the painted portraits, by Andrea Salmincio, appears in Imperialis's *Musæum Historicum et Physicum*, published at Venice in 1640. It resembles the others in facial type.

PLATE XVIII
GEORGE BUCHANAN
1506–1582

Painter and date: unknown.
Size: panel 18 × 11 ins.
In the possession of the UNIVERSITY OF EDINBURGH.

GEORGE BUCHANAN, the third son of a Stirlingshire farmer, who dying young left his family poorly provided for, had received the groundwork of his education in the schools of his own country, when, at the age of fourteen, a brother of his mother's sent him to the University of Paris. Only two years later, however, his uncle died and he had to return home; but, after a border campaign with the Regent Albany's army, he went to St. Andrews to complete his course and take his degree (1525). A year later he returned to Paris, and, in spite of many hardships, devoting himself to study and scholarship, graduated M.A. at the Scots College, and was appointed a regent in the College of Ste. Barbe, where he greatly improved instruction in the classics and produced a translation of Linacre's Grammar. In 1530 he was selected elector for the 'German' nation, but in the following year severed his connection with the University to become tutor to the Earl of Cassillis. By 1535, when he wrote a poem 'Somnium,' which gave dire offence to the Franciscans, he was back in Scotland, but appointment as tutor to a natural son of James V. led to further satires on the Grey-Friars, which resulted in his having to leave home once more. He then became regent in the College de Cuyenne at Bordeaux, where he had Montaigne as a pupil. There he also wrote many occasional pieces and several tragedies. Buchanan is next heard of (1547) as a colleague of Gouvéa in the Portugese College of Coimbra, but, falling into the hands of the Inquisition, he was imprisoned for nearly two years, and on regaining his liberty sailed for England. England was only a stepping-stone to France, 'Happy France, kind nurse of all the arts of life,' as he addressed her in a poem of this time, where he became tutor to the son of the great Maréchal,

50

GEORGE BUCHANAN

the Comte de Brissac, then in command of the French forces in Italy. In 1561, however, he returned to Scotland and almost immediately we learn, from a letter of Randolph's, that 'The Queen [Mary] readeth daily after her dinner, instructed by a learned man, Mr. George Bowhannan, somewhat of Lyvie'; and, a little later, he was appointed translator of foreign correspondence. He also wrote poems and masques for the court. Yet he had definitely joined the Reformation party and took an active part in the organisation of the Kirk. In 1566 the Earl of Moray made him principal of the College of St. Leonard, St. Andrews, and the following year he was, though a layman, Moderator of the General Assembly. After the murder of Darnley and Mary's marriage to Bothwell, he lost all regard for the Queen; the 'Detectio,' supposed to have been drawn up by him on the instructions of the Privy Council, is a most serious indictment of her actions, and he accompanied the Scottish Commissioners to London in 1568. In 1570, a year after he became tutor to the young King, he was appointed Keeper of the Privy Seal. *De Jure Regni*, in which the rights and duties of kings and subjects are discussed in a remarkably free manner, appeared in 1579, and this was followed by his last and greatest work, *Rerum Scoticarum Historia* (1580). Almost all he wrote was in Latin, of which he was accounted the greatest contemporary master.

Humanist and reformer, he was an incarnation of the opposing forces and tendencies of the transition times in which he lived. In many respects also his career is typical of his country and its people. By energy of character, concentration of purpose, and devotion to duty, he raised himself from poor and unpromising surroundings to a commanding position and influenced the thought and scholarship of his age.

WHILE no contemporary proof of the authenticity of any portrait of Buchanan, such as has assured the Beza woodcut of Knox, has been forthcoming, the engraving, which from the initials upon it may be by Jacques Granthomme, in Boisards's *Icones Vivorum Illustrium* (Frankfort, 1598) is probably founded upon an authentic likeness. Sir William Hamilton compared various portraits of Buchanan by measurement with the skull preserved in the University of Edinburgh as his, and this engraving stood the test. With it Sir William classed, as conforming to the standard, an old portrait, which has been in the possession of the same University probably from the time of its foundation, and when James Drummond, R.S.A., made his investigation of the portraits of Knox and Buchanan, he also accepted it as genuine. Painted on fir panel in a rather archaic style, it is a contemporary work, and, from internal evidence, an excellent likeness. The modelling, specially of the upper part of the face, is, if somewhat halting, such as one does not find usually in a copy: the structure of the facial bones is definite and the wrinkles about the eyes are full of character. The mouth and chin are less convincing, and do not resemble the engraving so closely as the other parts, but they have been retouched, and the portrait does not represent quite so old a man. In both picture and engraving the eyes have a marked character, and those in the print suggest quite clearly the colour one finds in the painting. One man is represented in both, and he is probably, almost certainly, George Buchanan. A second picture in the Edinburgh senate-room is much less interesting, and, while in some respects liker the engraving, is marked by the emptiness characteristic of a copy at several removes. With it may be placed the standing half-length in the London Portrait Gallery. Of higher artistic merit, it yet belongs to the same class, and it bears the same inscription.

A portrait by Frans Pourbus, the elder (1545-1581), in the possession of the Royal Society (London), is also supposed to represent Buchanan. It belonged to Dr. Mead in 1741, when Houbraken engraved it, and, presented to the Society by T. Povey, it possesses considerable claims to consideration. The head is rounder and shorter in type and flabbier in structure, and the clear grey eyes are wanting, but considering the great range possible in authentic portraiture, it may well be a portrait of Buchanan, whom Pourbus could have painted during one of the Scot's many visits to the Continent. Numerous copies of this type exist.

It would have been unnecessary to say anything of Lord Buchan's Titian portrait had the Buchanan Society not had it reproduced within recent years from the copy the Earl got Raeburn to make for him. As Drummond relates, in the monograph already referred to, it was exposed to the Earl himself by a friend, who showed him the same portrait engraved, in an important French work published more than a hundred years before his lordship made his great discovery, as a likeness of Jeannin, Finance Minister to Henri iv.

52

GEORGE 3RD LORD SETON & HIS FAMILY

PLATE XIX

GEORGE, 5TH LORD SETON AND HIS FAMILY

Painter: unknown, after an original attributed to Sir Antonio More (1512?-1576?), and understood to belong to the representatives of the last Lord Somerville.
Date of original: 1569.
Size: 48½ × 32 ins.
In the possession of G. S. Hay, Esq.

AMONGST her nobles, Mary Stuart had no more devoted subject than 'The Loyal Seton.' From the time he acted as one of the commissioners to witness her marriage with the Dauphin in 1558 until her cause became quite hopeless, he worked and plotted and fought for her. He was the eldest son of the fourth Lord of his name, and, remaining a Catholic, went to France for a time after the triumph of Protestantism; but he was back in Scotland before Queen Mary and was appointed Master of the Household and sworn a Privy Councillor. A quarrel with Secretary Lethington led to another visit to France, but soon he was recalled, and after Rizzio's murder the Queen fled to Seton House. To Seton also she went after Darnley's murder, and even after the Bothwell marriage he remained faithful. He was waiting to receive her when she escaped from Lochleven (May 1568) and was one of the leaders at Langside, where he was taken prisoner. Without giving up her cause, he was now less active in it, but it was 1579 before he definitely acknowledged the young King. He opposed the Regent Morton, and when that noble fell he and his sons witnessed the execution. Latterly he was in James's favour, and just before his death was sent on an embassy to France.

LORD SETON (1530-1585) married Isabel Hamilton, daughter of the High Treasurer of Scotland, and had one daughter, Margaret, who married Lord Claud Hamilton (Lord Paisley) in 1574 and became ancestress of the Dukes of Abercorn, and five sons, the eldest of whom died in March 1562 and, with

53

his mother, does not figure in this picture, which was painted some seven years later. The others are Robert, Master of Seton, afterwards 6th Lord Seton, who was created Earl of Winton by King James VI.; Sir John Seton, Lord Barns; Alexander Seton, Prior of Pluscardine, afterwards Chancellor of Scotland and Earl of Dunfermline (1555 ?-1622); and Sir William Seton of Kyllismore, Sheriff of Mid-Lothian. The inscription 'Chansler Seton, Earl Dunfermlin' (and probably the 'George, Lord Seton'), is a later addition, and has been placed on the wrong figure: that to the right, with 'A. S., 14,' over the head, is the Chancellor.

Several versions of this picture, the original of which is said to have been painted by Sir Antonio More when on a visit to Lord Seton at Seton House, where it was greatly admired by Charles I., exist, but that reproduced is understood to be the best and in the best condition. It is possibly that referred to by Sir George Chalmers, the painter, in *The Bee* (1798) as being a copy by a French artist, and it is supposed to have come from Seton. As More was in England in 1553, and for a short time only, and settled for good in Antwerp about 1568, while the original of the Seton family group must have been painted about 1569, the tradition referred to rests on a very slender foundation and cannot be accepted.

Another portrait of Lord Seton, attributed to Holbein, is believed to be in the possession of the representatives of the last Lord Somerville; and interesting miniatures of him and his lady appear in an armorial pedigree at Touch, dated 1585. A portrait of the Chancellor dated 1610, when he was fifty-five, is at Yester; another is mentioned in Mr. George Seton's history of the family (1896) as belonging to Mrs. Coventry, Burgate House.

MARY QUEEN OF SCOTS

MARY QUEEN OF SCOTS

1542–1587

XX. Draughtsman: François Clouet (1518?–1573?).
Date: 1558.
In the Bibliothèque Nationale, Paris.

XXI. Painter and date: unknown.
Size: panel 45×30 ins.
In the possession of the EARL OF MORTON.

BORN in Linlithgow Palace, on 7th or 8th December 1542, when her father, James V., lay dying, killed by the shame of Solway Moss, except for the brief bright years of her youth in France, Mary Stuart lived in an atmosphere of tragedy and gloom. It was in July 1548 that the Estates ratified a treaty for her marriage with the Dauphin, son of Henri II., and in the following month she sailed for France, where she was educated with the Royal children and brought up in the midst of the most brilliant court in Europe. There, in Notre-Dame, she was married (24th April 1558), after having signed away the liberty of her own country; but the death of her sickly husband, less than a year and a half after his succession to the throne, upset all her ambitious dreams of sovereignty over Scotland, France, and England, and she bade a passionate farewell to France. Arrived in Scotland, she found the reformed religion in the ascendant and reluctantly left it undisturbed. The conduct of affairs remained with her half-brother, Lord James Stuart, whom she created Earl of Moray, and Maitland of Lethington, and her relations with Queen Elizabeth, whom she had hurt grievously by her claims to the English crown when Queen of France, improved. After numerous projects of marriage had been abandoned owing to international jealousies, Mary herself decided to marry Henry Stuart, Lord Darnley, a grandson of Queen Margaret Tudor and next heir after herself to the throne of England. As he was the Queen's second cousin, a papal dispensation was necessary, but, although an envoy from

55

SCOTTISH PORTRAITS

Rome was supposed to have brought it, he had not, and Mary, suppressing the fact, married without the Pope's consent (29th July 1565). She now showed her favour for Catholicism more openly, and after the 'Round-about' raid Moray and other Protestants took refuge in England. Meanwhile Darnley had turned out quite unworthy, and his jealousy of Rizzio made him a willing accomplice of the Lords, who had decided to remove the Italian secretary. But his share in the plot being disclosed, he sank still farther in the Queen's esteem, and even the birth of a son (James VI.) led to a seeming reconciliation only. Bothwell, who had aided Mary against Moray, was now in great favour, and when the Queen brought her husband, who had been sick in Glasgow, to Edinburgh, it was Bothwell who conveyed him to the Kirk-o'-Field. A few days later (10th February 1567) the house was blown up, and the King found murdered. A sham trial followed, and then, after some little show of resistance, Mary married Bothwell—in the Protestant form. But her barons rose in arms, and at Carberry Hill, after securing Bothwell's retreat, she surrendered at discretion and was sent to Lochleven Castle, where she was forced to demit her crown in favour of her son. Some months later, acting in concert with the Hamiltons, she escaped; but her army being defeated by the Regent Moray, she fled southward, and, crossing the Solway in an open boat, sought refuge in England. To the English Queen, however, she was no welcome guest, and after many plottings for restoration to Scotland and against Elizabeth, and many weary years in prison, she was executed at Fotheringay on 8th February 1587. And so, as Sainte-Beuve says in his fine essay, 'Elizabeth living, triumphed, and her policy, after her, still triumphs and obtains, so that Protestantism and the British Empire are one and the same thing. Mary Stuart fell in her own person and in that of her descendants; Charles I. under the axe, James II. in exile carried on and increased her heritage of error, imprudence, and disaster; the whole race was cut off, and seems to have deserved its fate. But though vanquished in the real order of things, in the empire of fact and inexorable reason, the beautiful Queen regained everything in the domain of imagination and pity. There, from century to century, she found knights, lovers, and avengers.'

AS might be expected from the surpassing interest of Mary Stuart's personality, the number of her portraits is legion. Yet close scrutiny of their claims reduce those that have a right to be considered reliable to comparatively few, and these well marked in type. They belong either to the years she was in France

56

or to the nineteen she spent in English prisons; but, whether early or late, they possess the same characteristics. Briefly, these are a clear pale complexion; red to ruddy-brown hair; eye varying from chestnut to hazel; an oval face, with a broad high forehead; a straight nose, drooping very slightly towards the point when seen in profile; an upper lip delicately moulded in her youth, but hard and thin in later years; a mouth of fully average width, with lips closed in the earlier and compressed in later portraits; and a well-developed but not strong chin. The eyebrows, of paler colour than her hair and rather weakly marked, are arched; the eyes, of less than average size, are keen but sly in expression, of almond shape, under thick eyelids, and lines drawn through them from the middle of the nose, are either horizontal or slope upwards. The effigy on the monument in Westminster is the sole exception to the last: in it the eyes droop towards their outer corners. And in several of her portraits there is a suggestion of a slight cast in her eyes. Sir James Melville records that her complexion was fair; Brantôme, describing her appearance when wearing the *blanc-atour*, or white habit of her youthful widowhood, says that the brilliant whiteness of her complexion was dazzling; and Beal, Clerk of the Privy Council, who was sent to report her execution, mentions that her eyes were chestnut colour. She was handsome and of 'the largest size.' It was remarked that the borrowed red petticoat which she wore at Carberry reached only to her knees.

While certain of Mary's features taken by themselves might be called beautiful, none of the authentic portraits shows what one may fairly call a beautiful woman. Her beauty, which she inherited from her father, must have depended very largely upon expression, colouring, and complexion; more probably still, it was the fascination of her personality which charmed her contemporaries and inspired their eulogies.

As adequate discussion of her portraits would require a volume, here it must suffice to tabulate the more important, excluding the coinage and suchlike, which in a fuller treatment would demand consideration.

PORTRAITS DATING BEFORE HER RETURN FROM FRANCE

A chalk drawing in red and black, in the Bibliothèque Nationale, previously in the Bibliothèque Ste. Geneviève, Paris, attributed to Clouet, and thought to be a study from life for the Windsor miniature. It is reproduced in this series. Date about 1558. Other two drawings, one now at Chantilly and both reproduced in Lord Ronald Sutherland Gower's splendid volumes on the Lenoir and Castle Howard collections, are somewhat similar in type.

The card miniature in colour, attributed to Clouet, at Windsor, for which the first drawing may be a study.

A drawing in red, black, and yellow crayons in the Bibliothèque Nationale, formerly in the Bibliothèque Ste. Geneviève, by Clouet, representing her in her widow's dress. Date 1560-1. In this she appears older than she could well have looked at that time, but this effect is to a great extent delusive and caused by the peculiarity of the costume.

An oil picture, on panel, of the above, was in Charles I.'s collection, and is now at Windsor. Repetitions are in the Wallace collection, the National Portrait, and Scottish National Portrait Galleries. Of these the last is probably the best.

As stated in the Introduction, the only record of Mary's appearance during her reign in Scotland is to be found on coins and medals. It was at Sheffield that the next authentic portrait was painted.

PORTRAITS DATING FROM HER CAPTIVITY IN ENGLAND

A life-size full-length at Harwick Hall, painted at Sheffield by P. Oudry in 1578. In this she appears worn and thin, and the expression of face is hard and sinister. She stands, beside a table and before a curtain, dressed in black with an elaborate ruff open in front; the front edge of her white cap is bowed down over the brow; and her long white muslin veil is wired out like wings over her shoulders. She has a cross, a crucifix, and a rosary. Unsigned versions of this portrait are at Hatfield, Cobham, and Welbeck, and a half-length, very similar and once in Charles I.'s collection, is in the National Portrait Gallery.

The 'Sheffield' portrait is probably the original of several important portraits of Mary, of which the 'Morton' at Dalmahoy and the imposing full-length at Hampton Court, attributed to Mytens, are the most notable. The latter was painted for James VI. or Charles I., and in it the figure is turned to the right, the opposite direction to the original. It is the source of many later copies. Lord Morton's picture, a three-quarter-length, is traditionally said to have been given by the Queen to George Douglas, who assisted her to escape from Lochleven in 1568, and to have passed from him to the 4th Earl of Morton, but, as has been pointed out, the dress contradicts the tradition, and the portrait resembles

58

the Sheffield one in type, although it presents several important variations from it, of which the absence of religious emblems, the action of the hands, and a distinct difference in the veil are the most notable. The face is like the Sheffield in type but more pleasing, and of all the reliable portraits of Mary it comes nearest being beautiful. The same costume, associated with a considerably younger face than that in the Harwick picture, occurs in an interesting portrait in the Hermitage, St. Petersburg. A three-quarter-length, it is the only seated portrait known, and the only one, except the Windsor miniature, in which she wears rings. The attribution to Clouet is more than doubtful.

The ' Memorial' portraits at Blairs College, Windsor Castle, and Cobham Hall, although in a strict sense not contemporary, are almost as reliable as if they had been painted from life. They represent her at full length, standing, robed in black, with a large white wheel ruff, a white cap bowed over the brows, and a long white muslin veil reaching to the ground. She holds a large crucifix of ivory and ebony and carries a vellum-bound prayer-book. Her face is fuller and older than in the Sheffield pictures. In the background to the left the execution is shown; to the right are the figures of her two attendants, Elizabeth Curle and Jane Kennedy; and in the upper left corner are the Scottish arms. The placing and details of these accessories vary in the three versions, of which that at Blairs is the best. Upon Elizabeth Curle's monument in Antwerp is a bust portrait taken from the Blairs picture, which once belonged to her. In it a crown has been clumsily added. Copies of this bust are not infrequent.

Finally, as supplying a reliable portrait of Mary Stuart in the round, there is the effigy on her tomb in Westminster Abbey, which was commissioned by her son, James VI. and I., before 1606, and for which the final payment for painting and gilding was made in 1616. Cornelius and William Cure were the sculptors, and James Mauncy the colourist.

In the preparation of this summary of the authentic portraits of Queen Mary the elaborate and learned discussion of her portraiture in Sir George Scharf's letters to *The Times* has been invaluable, and for the information of those who wish to study his conclusions in their entirety, the dates on which they appeared are February 7, May 7, October 80, and December 26, 1888.

PLATE XXII
JOHN NAPIER OF MERCHISTON
1550–1617

Painter : unknown.
Date : 1616.
Size : 46½ × 38¾ ins.
In the possession of the UNIVERSITY OF EDINBURGH.

LITTLE is known of the early life of this great mathematician except that he was the eldest son of Sir Archibald Napier of Merchiston, where he was born, and was educated at St. Andrews and in the Netherlands, France, and Italy. By 1571 he had returned, and shortly afterwards he married Elizabeth, daughter of Sir James Stirling of Keir, and settled at Gartnes on the Endrick, where he lived until 1608, when he succeeded his father and removed to Merchiston. As a laird he gave considerable attention to improvements in agriculture, and he introduced a new method of pumping water from collieries. For some years also he took an active interest in theological questions and wrote a book on 'Revelation,' directed against the Catholic apologists, which went through several English editions and was translated into three or four languages. But he was devoted principally to mathematics, in which he made notable discoveries. After many years' close application he gave the results of his studies to the world in *Mirifici Logarithmorum Canonis Descriptio* (1614), an elaboration of the *Constructio*, written a considerable time before. It was received with enthusiasm, for mathematicians at once saw the immensely increased power of calculation introduced by the new tables. The *Constructio*, which explains the method of constructing the tables, was not published until two years later. He also wrote a book (published 1617) explaining the use of a calculating machine, consisting of a series of little ivory rods and known in consequence as 'Napier's bones,' which he had invented. ' Napier's place among great originators in mathematics is fully acknowledged and the improvements that he introduced constitute an epoch in the history

60

JOHN NAPIER OF MERCHISTON
1550 - 1617

JOHN NAPIER OF MERCHISTON

of the science. He was the earliest British writer to make a contribution of commanding value to the progress of mathematics.'

THE portrait reproduced was painted in the year preceding Napier's death, and was presented to Edinburgh University by Margaret, Baroness Napier, his great-granddaughter, who succeeded to the title in her own right in 1686. In the upper right corner is 'Ætatis 66'; in the opposite are his arms, initials, and the date 1616, and below these 'In prudentia et simplicitate' is inscribed on a white ribbon, above which the source of the quotation, 'Math. 10. 16.,' is marked, while below, to the left, a serpent, and, to the right, a dove are painted. He wears a costume of black and grey, with white ruff and wrist-bands, and sits in a chair upholstered in red and black. His hair and beard are brown, and his eyes warm dark grey. In addition to the book seen in the reproduction, there can be made out dimly in the picture itself other books, a pair of compasses, and a globe on a red-covered table to the left.

A portrait, similar in size, belongs to Lord Napier and Ettrick and has always been in the family. In it he is seated also, but the attitude, dress and chair are somewhat different, and he wears a black cowl which conceals the hair and half the brow. Mark Napier, in his *Memoirs of Napier of Merchiston*, says that, though quaint and interesting, it is a ruder specimen of art, emptier in modelling and not nearly so well painted. It was engraved for *De Arte Logistica* (1889), and several copies exist. An engraving (Francesco Delaram, fecit and sculp.), dated 1620, shows him as a younger (?) man, with a moustache and a close-cropped pointed beard. The face is much less refined than in the pictures, and the position (he is represented using his 'bones') is very cramped. Very poor as an engraving, it is of little account as a portrait.

PLATE XXIII

GEORGE HERIOT

1563–1624

Painter: JOHN SCOUGALL (1645 ?-1730 ?), after Paul Van Somer (1576-1621).
Date: 1698.
Size: 50¼ × 38 ins.
In the possession of the GOVERNORS OF HERIOT'S HOSPITAL, Edinburgh.

GEORGE HERIOT was brought up to the business of his father, a goldsmith in Edinburgh, who, when his son married in 1586, set him up in a business of his own. Two years later he joined the incorporation of his craft, and only six years after that he was chosen a convener of the trades of the city. In 1597 he became goldsmith to Queen Anne of Denmark, and in April 1601 jeweller to the King. But in reality he was much more, and again and again advanced money to them. He followed the court to London at the time of the Union, and, being appointed 'His Majesty's Jeweller,' soon had such a large business that it was with difficulty he found sufficient workmen. Thus he accumulated a fortune which, after the death of his second wife, Alison Primrose, an aunt of the first Earl of Rosebery, he willed to his native city to found the Hospital which bears his name. A capital sum of £23,625 in 1624, when he died, it yielded an annual income of £24,000 in 1880, and the revenue continues to increase. The Hospital itself is devoted to a school, partly technical in character, and the Trust also controls and finances the Heriot-Watt College.

'As 'Jingling Geordie,' Heriot is a principal figure in Sir Walter Scott's *Fortunes of Nigel.*

HERIOT'S HOSPITAL has a portrait of the founder painted in his twenty-sixth year, but it is much less interesting than that reproduced, which was copied by John Scougall in 1698 from the now lost original by Paul van Somer, the favourite artist of James VI. It possesses considerable character and

62

GEORGE HERIOT

GEORGE HERIOT

may be accepted as an excellent likeness of the founder of the Hospital in which it hangs. It shows him, dressed in a black doublet and a black cloak lined with a richly flowered green stuff, standing, holding a medal, before a red-patterned curtain; a heavy pillar appears to the right, and before it a number of jewels lie on a red-covered table. He has a ruddy complexion, short yellow-brown hair and beard, and dark blue eyes.

PLATE XXIV

LADY JEAN GORDON

COUNTESS OF BOTHWELL, AND AFTERWARDS OF SUTHERLAND

1544–1629

Painter: GEORGE JAMESONE (d. 1644).
Size: 26 × 19½ ins.
In the possession of the DUKE OF SUTHERLAND, K.G., K.T.

THE third daughter of the Earl of Huntly—the greatest of Mary Stuart's Catholic subjects—who fell at Corrichie (1562), Lady Jean Gordon was married to James Hepburn, Earl of Bothwell, in February 1566; but immediately after Darnley's murder, a year later, the Earl, anticipating that the Queen would gratify his ambition, applied for a divorce on the ground that, although within the prohibited degree, they had been married without a dispensation. It appears that the lady had received the necessary permission (the deed is preserved in the Sutherland charter chest), but probably she was glad to be rid of her lawless husband and did not produce it. Bothwell then married the Queen (May 1567), and Lady Jean retired to Strathbogie. Later she married the young Earl of Sutherland, who died in 1594, and five years later she took Alexander Ogilvie of Boyne, the widower of Mary Beaton, as her third husband, and, living till 1629, survived him also. She had a family by the Earl of Sutherland, and her son, Sir Robert Gordon, historian of that family, speaks of her as 'a vertuous and comlie lady, judicious, of excellent memorie, and of great understanding above the capacitie of her sex.'

MR. BULLOCH, biographer of George Jamesone, examined this picture at Dunrobin, and refers to it as follows. It is No. 181 in his list of Jameson's portraits.

'So far, however, as size, drawing, and pose reveal anything, it is that

64

LADY JEAN GORDON

Jamesone was the artist. Lady Jean is attired in a bonnet, with the deep veil of a widow—a widow for the third time. She is seated, and the high chair forms a sort of background. The features are rather marked and exhibit a character of firmness but not one devoid of feeling. The mouth is quite in Jamesone's manner. The face is very pale and the hair perfectly silvered. Lady Jean, who clung tenaciously to the old faith, wears a rosary which is suspended in her right hand, on the *back* of which an attached cross lies.'

PLATE XXV

PATRICK FORBES OF CORSE

BISHOP OF ABERDEEN

1564–1635

Painter and date: unknown.
Size: panel 27¾ × 22⅝ ins.
In the possession of the SENATUS ACADEMICUS OF ABERDEEN UNIVERSITY
(Marischal College).
Photographic negative lent by the NEW SPALDING CLUB, Aberdeen.

PATRICK, eldest son of William Forbes, Laird of Corse, was born in Aberdeen, but received his education in Stirling and at Glasgow and St. Andrews Universities under his kinsman Andrew Melville, with whom he also visited Oxford and Cambridge (1584-5). While yet young he was offered a divinity chair, but declined; and on his father's death, and some eight or nine years after his marriage, he settled at Corse, where he attended to his estates without discontinuing his theological studies. At last, in 1612, he agreed to be ordained minister of Keith parish, and six years later, being nominated episcopal Bishop of Aberdeen, reluctantly consented to be consecrated. As Bishop he was a conspicuous success, and was loved and respected throughout his diocese, and indeed wherever he was known. Forbes, who had conformed to James VI.'s moderate Episcopacy, strongly opposed Charles I.'s attempt to thrust the English system on Scotland, but in 1632 he was laid partially aside, and three years later he died. The colleges of Aberdeen owed much to him, and he has been compared to Bishop Elphinstone, one of the greatest cleric-statesmen of pre-Reformation Scotland, and his most illustrious predecessor in the diocese and in the Chancellorship of King's College.

LITTLE need be said about this, the best and most reliable portrait of Bishop Forbes, except that he has rich brown eyes, grey hair, and a dark grey beard, and wears a black cap and gown and a white ruff. Like most good, and many bad, Scottish portraits of this period, it has been ascribed to Jamesone, but examination does not bear out the attribution, and it is more probably the work of a Dutch painter, or, at least, of a follower of the Dutch school. Jamesone indeed painted Forbes, but his picture, in Lord Sempil's possession at Fintray House, has been restored and rendered uninteresting. The engraving in *Funerals,* the memorial volume, published shortly after his death, in which many eminent Scotsmen paid the Bishop tribute, although it prints reverse, is evidently founded on the Marischal College portrait (there is an inferior version in King's), but it is an indifferent piece of work, probably by Robert Gaywood, whose initials it bears.

SIR WILLIAM ALEXANDER, EARL OF STIRLING

W

home Will...
travelled wit...
t, m his r...
...n with the...
...d James...
...tGoS...
...

...

...

...

...

...he...

...de men...

...a save knew...

...King expow...

...wak the new...

...and the proje...

...become Secret ry for...

...nt on the...

PLATE XXVI

SIR WILLIAM ALEXANDER
EARL OF STIRLING

1580 ?-1640

Painter: unknown.
Date: ' Ætatis su. LVII.'
Size: 28 × 20¾ ins.
In the possession of LIEUT.-COLONEL ALEXANDER.

WHILE the Alexanders of Menstrie claimed descent from Somerled, Lord of the Isles, it was not until the close of the sixteenth century that they produced a man of real distinction. Born in the ancestral home, William Alexander, after attending Glasgow and Leyden Universities, travelled with his kinsman the seventh Earl of Argyll in Spain, Italy, and France, and, on his return, was chosen tutor to Prince Henry. He made his *début* as an author with the *Tragedie of Darius*, published in Edinburgh in 1603, and then followed James VI. and the Scottish Court to London. Darius was succeeded by *Aurora* (1604), a collection of love sonnets written at an earlier date and partly autobiographical in character; by *A Paraeneses to the Prince*, and by other tragedies; and Alexander made friends with Drayton and Aytoun. Drummond of Hawthornden he, of course, knew, and a charming letter, written by the younger poet, describes a visit to Menstrie in 1614. But he was more than a courtier or even a poet: he filled several great offices of state with credit and was one of the most versatile men of his generation. His was the idea of colonising that part of North America since known as Nova Scotia with Scottish emigrants, and to aid the scheme the King empowered him to create, for a consideration, Nova Scotia baronets; but, while the new titles proved attractive, Scotland was not ripe for colonial expansion, and the project failed.

In 1626 he became Secretary for Scotland, four years later he was created Viscount Stirling, and on the occasion of Charles's Scottish coronation he was advanced to an earldom.   About this time also he built that fine old Stirling mansion, Argyll Lodge.   But in old age he fell on evil days; his two sons died within a year, his fortunes declined, and he died bankrupt in London.   Three years before the end he collected his writings, and published them with the title *Recreations with the Muses.*   From the portrait in that book it has been conjectured that he was born in 1580, but the plate is undated, and 1567 is regarded as a more probable date.

THE earliest portrait of Stirling is the engraving which appeared in the third edition of his *Monarchicke Tragedies*, published in London in 1616.   It is a somewhat rude performance, but the face, although younger and thinner and more pointed, bears considerable resemblance to the very rare folio print which prefixed the earl's *Recreations with the Muses* in 1637.   The latter, engraved by W. Marshall and considered one of his best performances, is encircled by a ribbon bearing this inscription, 'Vera effigies Gulielmi Comit. de Sterlin. Ætatis su. LVII,' which, if the print be contemporary with its publication, would make his birth year 1580, and, although other circumstances seem to point to his having been born at least a decade earlier, the reference to the earldom would seem to indicate that it belongs to after 1633.   The picture reproduced, which is in the possession of a branch of the Stirling family, bears a marked resemblance to the later engraving, which may well have been taken from it.   He has black hair, very dark brown beard and moustache and very dark eyes; his ruff is white and his doublet tawny.

PLATE XXVII

REV. ALEXANDER HENDERSON

1583-1646

Attributed to VAN DYCK.
Date of original source : about 1641.
In the possession of the MARQUIS OF TWEEDDALE, K.T.

BORN in Fifeshire, Henderson was sent to St. Andrews, where he so distinguished himself that he was appointed Professor of Philosophy and Rhetoric in 1610. A few years later, and just after James VI. had introduced a mild form of Episcopacy into Scotland, Archbishop Gladstanes forced him on Leuchars parish, but ere long his nominee had become a confirmed Presbyterian, and, in the Assembly of 1618, denounced the Five Articles of Perth. Gradually he was accorded a more and more important place in the councils of the Kirk. He opposed the Service-Book in 1637, was responsible in great measure for the National Covenant of 1638, and presided over the Assembly which abolished Episcopacy. When Charles I. visited Scotland in 1641, Henderson, who had been active in the negotiations which closed the first and second Bishops' Wars, acted as his chaplain, and succeeded in securing various advantages for Edinburgh University, of which he had been elected Rector during the previous year. That famous engagement between the Parliaments of England and Scotland, the 'Solemn League and Covenant,' was introduced by him to the Assembly of 1643, when he acted as Moderator for the third time, and from 1643 to 1646, he was a leading member of the Westminster Assembly, whence subsequently proceeded the Shorter Catechism and the Confession of Faith. His attempts to mediate between the King and his English Parliament were unsuccessful, and Charles surrendered to the Scots army at Newcastle, where he and Henderson had many discussions as to the rival claims of Episcopacy and Presbytery. But Henderson's health was failing, and he returned to Scotland to die only eight days later.

His able leadership and determined attitude towards the innovations and

71

arbitrary actions of James vi. and Charles i. did much to ensure the ultimate triumph of Presbyterianism in Scotland, and his statesmanship had a share in influencing the political destinies, not only of his own country, but of England also. In the Assembly of 1647, Baillie pronounced him 'the fairest ornament, after Mr. John Knox, of incomparable memory, that ever the Church of Scotland did enjoy.'

WHILE it is probable that the etching, executed by W. Hollar in 1641, is the most reliable portrait of Henderson, the admirable picture in Lord Tweeddale's collection lends itself more readily to reproduction and conveys with vividness the strongly marked features and much wrinkled brows of the great Covenanter. How it came to Yester is uncertain, but Bishop Pocock saw it there in 1760, when, as now, Van Dyck's name was associated with it. But, although an excellent piece of work, it has no clear claim to that attribution, and is more likely by a Dutchman of the later seventeenth century after Hollar's print. It gives the eyes as dark brown, the hair black, and the beard dark iron-grey. The Yester portrait is one of six mentioned by Aiton in his *Life of Henderson* (1836), and like it the others seem to derive from the etching. Those then at Hamilton Palace and Duff House were attributed to Jamesone, but the former, mentioned by Pennant in his *Tour in Scotland* (1769), has been entirely repainted, and the latter was sold a good many years ago as of little value. Others belong to Glasgow and Edinburgh Universities.

WILLIAM FEILDING 1ST EARL OF DENBIGH

PLATE XXVIII

WILLIAM DRUMMOND OF HAWTHORNDEN

1585–1649

Painter: CORNELIUS JONSON VAN CUELEN (1590?-1665
Date: 1612.
Size: panel 23¼ × 18½ ins.
In the possession of the EARL OF HOME, K.T.

THE outstanding figure in Scottish literature during the seventeenth century is William Drummond, but by the irony of fate his muse was more English than Scots. Born in Hawthornden, and educated at Edinburgh University, he studied law in France, and lived a good deal out of Scotland before 1610, when he succeeded his father, Sir John. But the death of his young wife, within a year of their marriage, unsettled him, and it was not until 1632, when he married again, that he settled for good at his romantic home above the Midlothian Esk. Meanwhile he had published an elegy on the death of the much - lamented Henry, Prince of Wales (1594-1612), *Poems* (1617), and *Flowers of Sion*, a volume of religious verse (1623), and in later years he wrote a *History of Scotland under the Five Jameses* (published posthumously) and other works in prose or verse. It is, however, to his sonnets and madrigals, which reveal great refinement of feeling and sensitiveness to the beauty of nature, and rank high in their kind, that he owes his place in letters, and his poetry, with that of his friend the Earl of Stirling, represents the influence of Elizabethan literature in Scotland. Michael Drayton and Ben Jonson, the latter of whom visited him at Hawthornden in the autumn of 1618, were also amongst his friends and correspondents. Public affairs interested him very little, but he was a devoted Royalist, and grief at the execution of Charles I. is said to have hastened his death.

SCOTTISH PORTRAITS

IF the old panel picture at Hawthornden is the best authenticated portrait of the poet, and is, in all probability, the source of the almost contemporary engravings by Gaywood, it has ceased to be more than interesting. J. G. Lockhart was delighted with it (see *Peter's Letters*) when he saw it some eighty years ago, and says that it was in fine condition; but since then it has been so much and so badly repainted that nothing but a rather ghastly ghost remains. And Gaywood's performances, especially the earlier, are no better. The folio of his *History*, which appeared in 1655, contains Gaywood's first attempt, and a sorry one it is. Drummond is like a scarecrow; but, despite the crudity of its execution and the fact that it prints reverse, the relationship of print to original is clear enough. *The Poems of that famous wit William Drummond of Hawthornden*, also published by Richard Tomlins (London: 1656 and 1659), is embellished with another and smaller print by the same engraver. It is much less hideous and liker the picture than its predecessor, and the figure is turned in the opposite direction. But it does not seem to have given satisfaction either, for it was retouched—and spoiled—for the 1681, 1682, and 1688 editions of Drummond's *History*. On the other hand, the Janssen is beautiful and expressive, and, although its history cannot be traced completely, it bears so close a resemblance to these rude effigies that it may be accepted as reliable. Dated 1612, it represents Drummond at the age of twenty-seven. As in the family picture, he has warm brown hair and very dark brown eyes, but his face is younger, fresher, and clean shaven. Why it was not chosen for his books will likely remain unsolved, but it may well be that it was thought to represent him at too early an age, and would be less familiar to his immediate contemporaries than the more recent portrait at Hawthornden. A miniature, then in the possession of the family, was engraved for an edition of the poems, which appeared in 1791, and for the Maitland Club issue of his works; but it shows him with a small pointed beard, a long curled moustache, and rather different features, and is difficult to reconcile with the portraits previously mentioned. Other portraits with more or less claim to represent Drummond are in the National Portrait Gallery, London, All Souls College, Oxford, and in the possession of Mr. Andrew Muirhead, and there is a miniature in the Buccleuch collection.

H

to Brodick
made Master
given the C...
in the war with...
to distinguish...
great favour...
Scotland a... C...
promises which...
country s, and...
ned. Alth...
us own preservation...
active measures before
there is no plea for delay...
... acquittal, and Char...
... where he remained unt...
... my 1646. He then
... after Charles had...
... ded him to raise a...
... England. But our...

73

PLATE XXIX

JAMES HAMILTON, 1st DUKE OF HAMILTON

1606–1649

Painter: Sir Anthony Van Dyck (1599-1641).
Size: 85 × 50 ins.
In the possession of the Trustees of the late Duke of Hamilton.

HAVING succeeded his father, the second Marquis, of whose death Buckingham was suspected, in 1625, he carried the sword at Charles i.'s coronation early in the following year, and then retired to Brodick, where he remained until 1628, when he was invited to Court and made Master of the Horse and a Privy Councillor. Two years later, he was given the Garter, and took some seven thousand men to help Gustavus Adolphus in the war with Germany; but he lost most of his troops and completely failed to distinguish himself. On his return, however, Charles, who regarded him with great favour, consulted him much on Scottish affairs, and in 1638 sent him to Scotland as Commissioner. But affairs there would not admit of the compromises which were all that Hamilton, divided between the King's, the country's, and, above all, his own interests, had the courage to suggest, and he resigned. Although Charles now knew that his favourite 'was very active in his own preservation,' he created him a Duke, and when Montrose advocated active measures before the Scots were fully prepared to take the field, Hamilton's plea for delay was acted upon. At last his failure to effect anything was too apparent, and Charles, unable to shelter Hamilton longer, sent him to prison, where he remained until St. Michael's Mount surrendered to the Parliamentary army (1646). He then set himself to secure Scottish support for the King, and, after Charles had been seized by the Independents, feeling in Scotland enabled him to raise a force of 10,000 or 12,000, with which he marched into England. But out-generalled, defeated, and taken prisoner by

SCOTTISH PORTRAITS

Cromwell at Preston, he was brought to trial, as Earl of Cambridge, condemned and executed a few months after his master.

IN the great Van Dyck of Charles I. in the Louvre, painted about 1635, and so familiar from engravings and reproductions, the Marquis of Hamilton, as he then was, appears as His Majesty's equerry, and his face, although somewhat younger (the hair also is lighter), is much the same as in the family portrait here reproduced. Many engravings, some of them contemporary, of the first Duke are clearly derived from the Hamilton Palace full-length (No. 588, Smith's Cat. Rais.), which shows him as a somewhat heavy faced man with dark brown eyes, dark brown hair in tangled locks, and lighter brown moustache and tuft. The Order of the Garter hangs about his neck; he is accoutred in full armour, wears buff boots, and carries a truncheon. At Hamilton there is also a most careful cabinet study (18 x 8 ins.) for this picture, of which the Duke of Buccleuch has a full-sized replica; and a three-quarter-length (47¼ x 37¾ ins.) in a black costume, by the same painter, and belonging to Lord Rosebery, shows a very similar face. Other portraits, attributed to Van Dyck, are in the collections of the Earls of Carlisle and Denbigh and at Knole. Still another was in the Clarendon Gallery, but it is now among the missing; and the two portraits in Holyrood, which bear his name, are really versions of Hanneman's rendering of the second Duke. Amongst engravings not after the Hamilton or Louvre pictures there is a very quaint print, representing him on horseback, in a book on Horsemanship, dedicated to the Duke and sold by ' Tho. Hind at the Black Bull in Cornhill'; but it is valueless as a likeness.

ALBERT DE ... MARQ ...

77

PLATE XXX

JAMES GRAHAM, MARQUIS
OF MONTROSE

1612–1650

Painter: WILLIAM DOBSON (1610-1646).
Date: 1644.
In the possession of the DUKE OF MONTROSE, K.T.

'CAVALIER *par excellence* of the Troubles,' as his biographer styles him, the Earl of Montrose began his career as a Covenanter. Young and ambitious and dissatisfied with his reception at Court, he joined the Presbyterian party and became an active supporter of the Covenant, which he forced the Episcopalians of the north to accept at the sword's point, and he took part in the first and second Bishops' Wars. But meeting Charles, he commenced to waver, and in 1643 offered to raise a Scottish force to support the King in his quarrel with the English Parliament. After a year's waiting, he was made a Marquis, and, receiving the Royal commission, embarked on his meteoric campaign. His army consisted of Highlanders and wild Irish troops, and, moving with incredible rapidity, it swept over the northern counties like a tornado and defeated force after force. At Tippermuir, Bridge of Dee, and Inverlochy, where he defeated the Campbells with great slaughter and sent his great enemy Argyll flying, at Auldearn, Alford, and Kilsyth, he won brilliant victories, and the last opening the Lowlands, he marched towards the Borders. But General David Leslie, with a picked force, had been summoned from England to meet him, and, surprising his army at Philiphaugh, routed it completely. Montrose fled to the Highlands, and thence to Holland; but in 1650 he was in Scotland again on Charles II.'s behalf. Ere long, however, his little band was cut to pieces, and he himself taken prisoner. Carried to Edinburgh, indignities were heaped upon him, and he was executed on the gallows. But he had shown high courage, and had dared 'to put it to the touch to win or lose

77

it all': he had sought glory and he found it—he lives in Scottish history as the 'Great Marquis.'

FOR years before his *Memoirs of Montrose* was published, Mark Napier (1798-1879) devoted himself to investigating, with a fervour quite religious in its intensity, every detail connected with the hero he worshipped as a saint. He examined almost every picture and print with pretensions to represent the Marquis, and ended in choosing four portraits as thoroughly reliable. And to his verdict little or nothing remains to be added. No portrait with serious claims has emerged in the interval, and with one exception the pictures remain with the families who owned them nearly forty years ago.

It was his fortune to be painted by good men, and, by an equally happy chance, the existing portraits show him as he was at each important crisis in his career.

The earliest was painted in November 1629, by George Jamesone, on the eve of the young Earl's marriage—he was only seventeen—to Magdalene, daughter of Lord Carnegie of Kinnaird (afterwards Earl of Southesk), and was taken during the following month to Kinnaird, where, or at least in the new castle of the same name, it still hangs. It is signed by the artist, whose signature is not often found on his pictures, dated, and gives the age of the sitter, whose fair boyish face—with its grey eyes, finely modelled nose, and delicate yet firm mouth—fringed with auburn hair of a lighter tone than later, has already the look one finds in the portraits of his maturity. Eleven years later, when swithering between Covenant and King, he sat a second time to the Aberdeen artist. Like the first, it shows him in the habit as he lived; the splendid wedding garments are replaced by a soldier's sleeveless buff coat over a satin doublet, and a sword-belt crosses his breast. The colour of the eyes is grey, but the hair is darker and cut straight across at the level of the eyebrows, and the face is less pleasing in expression and less well drawn. Painted for the Colquhouns of Camstraddan, it remained in their possession until some years ago, when it was acquired for the Duke of Montrose. The third portrait also belongs to the family, and has probably been in its possession always. Tradition attributes it to Van Dyck, but Mark Napier has demonstrated the improbability of this, and the ascription to Dobson, with the date 1644, is much more likely. Technically it is liker the English painter's style, and the symbolic accessories are quite in his vein. A fine bit of work, admirable in colour, in handling, and in expression, the awkwardness

78

JAMES GRAHAM, MARQUIS OF MONTROSE

of the design suggests that it is part of a larger canvas, and examination confirms the supposition. But even so it remains a noble portrait, and probably conveys a truer impression of the man than any other rendering. Here again the hair is brown and the eyes dark grey. The face, however, is fuller and rounder.

Finally, there is the poetic and impressive three-quarter-length, which belongs to the Earl of Dalhousie. Painted by Honthorst (1590-1656) in 1649—for the lovely and unfortunate Queen of Bohemia, who earned the more than Royal title, 'Queen of Hearts,' when, a few months after her father's, Charles I.'s, execution, Montrose received his commission as Lieutenant-Governor of Scotland from Charles II.—it reveals him on the very verge of the expedition which ended in his execution. He wears black armour, and the picture, except the face, is pitched in a sombre key: the whole conveys an impression of present mourning and impending doom. It is the Montrose of romance and legend, perhaps even of reality. Several excellent old versions of the Honthorst exist, but of the others there seems to be none of nearly the same age.

To these notes on the most reliable portraits of Montrose there may be added this pen-portrait by his faithful follower, Saintserf: 'He was of a middle stature, and most exquisitely proportioned limbs; his hair of light chesnut; his complexion betwixt pale and ruddy, his eye most penetrating, though inclining to grey; his nose rather aquiline than otherwise; as he was strong of body and limbs, so was he most agile, which made him excel most others in those exercises where these two are required.' A second description appears in *Montrose Redivivus* (1652), and confirms the other in almost every detail. 'He was,' it says, 'a man not very tall, nor much exceeding middle stature; but of exceeding strong composition of body and incredible force, with excellent proportion and feature; dark brown hair; sanguine complexion; a swift and piercing grey eye; with a high nose, something like the ancient sign of the Persian King's magnanimity.'

PLATE XXXI

ARCHIBALD CAMPBELL
MARQUIS OF ARGYLL

1598–1661

Painter: George Jamesone (d. 1644).
Size: 29¼ × 24¼ ins.
In the possession of the Marquis of Lothian.

JUST before the seventh Earl of Argyll (1576?-1638) declared himself a
Catholic in 1619, he transferred his estates to his eldest son, the Lord of
Lorn, who thus came to occupy a position of great power at an early
age. It was not, however, until Charles I. attempted to thrust the Service-
Book on Scotland and the Covenant was renewed (1638), that the young Earl,
who had succeeded to the title that year, allied himself openly with the
national party, in which he soon acquired enormous influence. He was active
in the negotiations between the King and the armed Covenanters at Duns
Law, and afterwards succeeded in having the bishops, suppressed by that treaty,
replaced by Lords of the Articles elected by the Estates themselves, and so
secured for Parliament the chief power in Scotland. In 1640, relations
between Charles and the Scots were again strained, and a Scots army
marched into England; but when the King visited Edinburgh a year later, the
demands of the Covenanters, engineered by Argyll, were acceded to, and he
was made a Marquis. Three years more saw Charles deep in the quarrel with
his English Parliament, the Scots once more in England, and Montrose openly on
the King's side. Argyllshire specially felt the wrath of Montrose; the Marquis
narrowly escaped capture at Inveraray, and his clansmen were defeated with
great slaughter at Inverlochy (1645), where he himself acted no creditable
part. When Philiphaugh closed Montrose's conquering career and the King
surrendered to the Scots army, Argyll's talent as a statesman came into play
again; but the execution of Charles threw everything into confusion, and

80

PLATE XXXI

ARCHIBALD CAMPBELL
MARQUIS OF ARGYLL

ARCHIBALD CAMPBELL MARQUIS OF ARGYLL

ARCHIBALD CAMPBELL

Argyll, whose career henceforward was shaped more by circumstances than himself, joined in inviting Charles II. to Scotland. He came a Covenanted King, but, although Argyll placed the crown on his head at Scone, the Hamilton party obtained the ascendency, and, against the Marquis's wish, marched an army into England, only to be defeated by Cromwell in the 'crowning mercy,' Worcester. A year later Argyll made his peace with the Protector, but his influence was gone and his fortunes ruined; and after the Restoration, when he sought an interview with Charles, he was arrested and sent to Edinburgh for trial. A conviction was required, and through the treachery of Monk, Cromwell's own lieutenant in Scotland, one was obtained, and Argyll was executed at Edinburgh Cross.

In the whole range of Scottish history there is no more fascinating and perplexing figure than the Marquis of Argyll. Others there are more brilliant, more convincing or more attractive, but scarcely another which presents so many facets or such a problem in character. He was, as the author of *John Splendid* puts it, two men in one skin. A born statesman, subtle in intellect, far-seeing and sagacious, he was lacking in the moral courage and the soldierly qualities which win willing admiration, yet in the end he rose above his timidity and died with a dignity and calmness which disconcerted his enemies and re-established him in the estimation of his friends.

DESPITE strongly marked facial characteristics, the presence of alien qualities in Argyll's character gives a wide range of expression to his portraits. That lost in the fire at Inveraray, and known as the 'Castle Campbell' portrait, because it was found in that neighbourhood, showed him as a comparatively young man, with lofty brow, in the middle of which his long dark brown hair was parted, lighter moustache, aquiline nose, short upper lip, close shut and slightly querulous mouth, and dark grey eyes with a suggestion of a squint. The expression was melancholy, but not sour as in later portraits, and he wore a broad white collar edged with lace, and over the right shoulder a white and gold scarf. In it he seemed more Cavalier than Covenanter, and a full-length at Dalkeith of rather earlier date (1680) resembles it in that and certain other respects. It is questionable, however, if the bust portrait engraved in Lodge—which, judging from the apparent age of the sitter, should be earlier than either—really represents him; and there is considerable doubt about a still more youthful portrait at Newbattle to which

81

his name has been attached.   While the features, and especially the rather sinister expression in the latter, suggest the Marquis as he might have been in early manhood, the exceeding fairness of the hair (the men of that period did not wear wigs) makes it difficult to reconcile with better authenticated portraits, and with the tradition which gives him ruddy hair.   The remaining portraits belong to a later period of his life.   Like the Castle Campbell picture, they have been attributed to Jamesone, and certainly that at Newbattle Abbey bears strong traces of his hand.   If that attribution is correct, it must have been painted before 1644, when Argyll was only forty-six, but, although one's first impression is that it represents an older man, examination shows that the face is more worn and weary than really aged, and in the luxuriant hair there is no hint of grey.   The Inveraray version was destroyed in 1877, but the photograph which registers its appearance corresponds with Lord Lothian's in all important respects.   The latter was probably brought to Newbattle along with the companion portrait of her mother by Argyll's daughter (wife of her cousin the first Marquis of Lothian), and now ranks as the best portrait of the Marquis.   In it the expression has become less open and more deeply melancholy, and the cast in the dark brown eyes is very distinctly marked.   The face is now clean shaven, the dark brown hair is brushed back from the brow and imprisoned under a close-fitting black skullcap, and the costume is puritanical in its severity.   These characteristics are exaggerated in the version of this portrait, which, once the property of Charles Kirkpatrick Sharpe, was presented to the Scottish National Portrait Gallery by the trustees of the late Sir William Fraser, and it was for that reason, perhaps, that Mark Napier chose it to represent Argyll in his book on Montrose.   But it is not, as Napier thought, by Jamesone, and may be set down as a rather later copy by an inferior hand.

From these portraits one understands why Argyll was spoken of in Lowland speech as the 'Glaed-eyed Marquis,' and was called 'Gillespie Grumach'—Archibald the Grim—by his Highland enemies.

ALEXANDER SEION, FIRST EARL OF EGLINTON

ALE.

PLATE XXXII

ALEXANDER LESLIE, 1st EARL OF LEVEN

1582 ?–1661

Painter: George Jamesone (d. 1644).
Date: 1635.
Size: 35 × 29 ins.
In the possession of Miss Leslie Melville.

LESLIE, who was born out of wedlock, early sought military employment abroad, and in 1605 joined the Swedish army, in which he served with great distinction. By 1626 he was lieutenant-general and a Swedish knight, and when two years later Gustavus Adolphus engaged in the Thirty Years' War, Leslie was given high command. After Gustavus was killed at Lützen (1632), he became general of the armies in Westphalia, and four years later succeeded Kniphausen as field-marshal. But Scotland now claimed his services, and he returned to take command of the Covenanting army in the approaching struggle with Charles I. There was no fighting in the first campaign, nor was the following in the north of England much more strenuous; and Leslie was created Earl of Leven when the King visited Scotland (1641). In July 1643, however, the English Parliament asked Scottish assistance in its quarrel with Charles, and, early in the next year, Leven led twenty thousand foot and two thousand horse into England, where they did yeoman service at Marston Moor and elsewhere. Charles surrendered to the Scottish army in 1645, and remained with Leven, who urged him to accept the Covenant and adopt a more liberal policy, until arrangements were made for his transference to the English Parliament. The Hamilton party then engaged to rescue the King, but Leven sided with Argyll against that policy, and, after its disastrous close at Preston, he and David Leslie raised a fresh army for home defence. He was present, but not in command, at Dunbar (1650), when David Leslie's plans were interfered with, and the Scots delivered themselves into Cromwell's hands. During the following year he was captured and sent to London; but, after being on parole for three years, he was given full liberty and his estates were restored. Leven then retired to his Fifeshire estate, where he died in 1661, aged about eighty.

AN inscription, ' 1635, Ætat. 53,' upon the canvas, indicates that it was painted during the General's visit to Scotland after the peace of Prague, and the jewel, with the miniature of Gustavus Adolphus, which he wears, is probably that given to him by the Swedish king in recognition of his services. The picture, therefore, represents Leslie as he was only a few years before he commenced to play his important part in national history. A very fair haired and bearded man, with dark blue eyes and fair pink complexion, the hair springs from well back on the brow, and falls in loose and thin locks on each side of a high and broad forehead, and the beard, clipped in stiff and formal fashion, seems to form a projection rather than an outgrowth from the chin. The head seems large for the figure, which bears out Baillie's description of him as an 'old, little, crooked souldier,' the littleness being very clearly shown by the position of the sword at his side. Its present owner inherited it from Leven's descendants, and in the list of pictures at Melville House, in Sir William Fraser's *The Leslies of Leven and the Melvilles of Melville*, where the relationship between the families is fully set forth, Jamesone is named as the painter, and, although uncharacteristic, it may be his work. The same may be said of a portrait of somewhat similar character, and of the same date, in Leslie House. The miniature, attributed to Cornelius Janssens and engraved in Pinkerton, probably represents him at an earlier age, to judge from costume and appearance before 1625. In it the complexion is rather ruddier and the hair browner; the eyes are again blue, and the moustache and chin tuft very fair; the brow is narrower, and the lower part of the cheeks fuller. It is, however, probably the same man as the other; but it is a less convincing rendering. A second miniature at Melville House confirms the colouring noted in the other portraits. Baron Rülamb of Granhammer, Sweden, has a full-length of the Scottish General, but it I have not seen.

PLATE XXXIII

SIR ARCHIBALD JOHNSTON

LORD WARRISTON

1610–1663

Painter: George Jamesone (d. 1644).
In the possession of Sir James H. Gibson-Craig, Baronet.

BORN in Edinburgh of Annandale stock, he became a pupil of Baillie at Glasgow, and in 1637, four years after he was admitted Advocate, was one of four counsel retained to advise the Kirk in its resistance to Charles I.'s ecclesiastical policy. Soon he obtained great influence, for he was at once a devoted Presbyterian and an able advocate, and he and Henderson drafted the amendments to the Covenant when it was renewed in 1638, while later in the same year he acted as Clerk to the Assembly, which abolished Episcopacy, and was appointed Procurator to the Kirk. Johnston was also engaged in the negotiations at Berwick and Ripon, and in 1641 Charles, having temporarily abandoned his pet scheme for Scotland, made him a knight and a Lord of Session with the title Lord Warriston. When the King's misunderstanding with the English Parliament reached a climax, Warriston served on the joint-committee appointed to supervise the military arrangements of the allies. He was a member of the Westminster Assembly of Divines also. Charles, while a prisoner in the Scottish camp at Newcastle, made him King's Advocate, but when the Engagers captured the Scottish Parliament he opposed the policy of rescue. Later he acquiesced reluctantly in the recall of Charles II., and, after the disaster at Dunbar, Cromwell deprived him of office. For some years Warriston opposed the Commonwealth, but in 1657 he again accepted the Lord-Clerk Registership, and, becoming one of Cromwell's peers, attained considerable influence under that Government. He was one of those marked for special punishment at the Restoration, but escaped, and decree of death and forfeiture was issued against him. Three years later,

85

an old and broken man, he was captured in France, sent to Edinburgh, and hanged.

JOHNSTON'S mother was the second daughter of Sir Thomas Craig of Riccarton, the great feudal lawyer, and the only known portrait of him belongs to the Riccarton family. An admirable example of Jamesone's simple and serious style and thin fluid method of painting (No. 64 in Mr. Bulloch's Catalogue), it represents him as a portly man of about forty, wearing a black velvet skullcap, from under which flows a profusion of soft, fair hair, hiding his ears and resting on the broad white collar which covers his shoulders.

SIR ARCHIBALD PRIMROSE, LORD CARRINGTON

PLATE XXXIV

SIR ARCHIBALD PRIMROSE

LORD CARRINGTON

1616–1679

Painter: JOHN SCOUGALL (1645 ?–1730 ?).
Date: 1670.
Size: 47 × 38½ ins.
In the possession of the EARL OF ROSEBERY, K.G., K.T.

IN 1641 Archibald Primrose succeeded his father as Clerk to the Privy
Council, but, after Montrose's last success at Kilsyth, he joined the
Royalists and was taken prisoner at Philiphaugh. Released in 1646, he
became one of the Engagers and accompanied Charles II. on his unfortunate
march to Worcester, with the result that, while he was created a baronet, his
estates were sequestrated, and he did not again hold office until the Restoration,
when he was made Lord-Clerk Register, a Lord of Session with the style
Lord Carrington, a Lord of the Exchequer, and a Privy Councillor. When
the Duke of Lauderdale supplanted Middleton, Carrington retained these offices,
but in 1676 the Registership was taken from him and given to a relation of the
Duchess, and he had to content himself with the position of Justice-General.
That, however, he was allowed to hold for two years only; and a year later he
died. It is from his only son by his second wife, Agnes, daughter of Sir William
Gray of Pittendrum, that the Earls of Rosebery are descended.

LORD ROSEBERY has two pictures of Lord Carrington, a bust portrait
(29¼ × 24¼ ins.), dated 1670, and the three-quarter-length reproduced, which
was acquired from the Rothes collection some years ago. Both are attributed
to Scougall, and in 1888 Lord Rosebery presented a copy of the smaller to the
Faculty of Advocates for the Parliament House. In these, and also in a seated
three-quarter-length at Penicuik, he wears the black and gold robes of his office
of Lord-Clerk Register, and has dark eyebrows, dark brown eyes, and a
brown wig. The Earl of Southesk and Lord Elphinstone possess portraits
of Carrington.

PLATE XXXV

JAMES SHARP

ARCHBISHOP OF ST. ANDREWS

1613–1679

Painter: Sir PETER LELY (1618-1680).
Date: about 1672.
In the possession of the EARL OF SOUTHESK, K.T.

JAMES SHARP, a native of Banffshire, who had been educated at Aberdeen and Oxford, was appointed Regent of Philosophy in St. Andrews University in 1648, and, four years later, he was presented to the parish of Crail by the Earl of Crawford. Soon he made himself one of the most prominent of that section of the Covenanters known as Resolutioners, and was delegated to represent them in London from 1656 to 1659. On the eve of the Restoration, Sharp was again selected to watch their interests and crossed to Breda to see the young King; but immediately he began to waver, and, returning to London, acted a double part, assuring his brethren in the North that their cause was safe in his hands, while in reality he was deep in the preparations for forcing Episcopacy upon Scotland. In August 1661 it was restored, and Sharp, rewarded for his apostasy by being made Archbishop of St. Andrews and Primate of Scotland, zealously co-operated with Middleton, the King's Commissioner, in its introduction. When Lauderdale superseded Middleton, Sharp had so played his cards that he retained place and influence, and in the terrible persecutions which followed he was a chief agent. Hated and despised by those he had first betrayed and then persecuted, he at length, and by mere chance, fell into the hands of several of the more desperate amongst them, and was murdered on Magus Moor.

THE best, as well as the best known, portrait of Sharp is that by Sir Peter Lely. Several replicas exist, and of these probably the finest is owned by Lord Southesk; but that shown by Lord Saltoun in the Exhibition of Scottish

PLATE XXXV

JAMES SHARP

ARCHBISHOP OF ST. ANDREWS

1613-1679

James Sharp, the son of a sheriff-clerk, was educated at Aberdeen, and became a regent or professor of Philosophy at St. Andrews University. About the year ——, he was presented to the parish of Crail by the —— Scot —— He was one of the most prominent of that —— party known as Resolutioners, and was delegated to cross —— to London at intervals. On the eve of the Restoration, Sharp —— the Presbyterian interests and crossed to that city to see the young —— was not —— Here, however, and on his way to London, he acted a —— by which the cause of the North —— this cause was safe in its —— by —— succeeding in the preparations for forcing Episcopacy —— on —— St. Andrews restored, and Sharp, rewarded for his —— as Archbishop of St. Andrews and Primate of Scotland —— in the High Commission court, in as much —— that he —— that —— conduct. The story —— so played its —— persecutions which —— by those who had —— at length, and by —— changes, fell into the —— young man amongst them, and was murdered on ——

—— as well as the best known portrait of Sharp is that by Sir Peter —— of these probably the finest is owned —— St. —— Lord Saltoun in the Exhibition of Scottish ——

JAMES SHARP

National Portraits (1884) is almost similar, and other versions, some only bust size, are of good quality. They unite in depicting him as a benevolent if rather crafty looking old man, with long white locks and dark grey eyes, wearing a black cap, white falling bands, and a black gown. Loggan's print—a bust— published four years before Sharp's death, is rather stiff and constipated in style, and has been taken either from life or a different original; but it bears considerable resemblance to the painted portraits, even to the wart on the under lip, and the pictures probably date a few years earlier. The face of his kneeling figure upon the elaborate black and white marble monument, executed in Holland and quite in the Dutch style, which was erected by his son in the Town Church of St. Andrews shortly after the murder, resembles these portraits, but is sharper and thinner. But the tradition which makes portraits of all the figures in the interesting relief, in which the tragedy which closed his career is represented, is of course not to be believed.

PLATE XXXVI

DUKES OF HAMILTON AND LAUDERDALE

Painter : Cornelius Jonson van Cuelen (1590 ?-1665).
Date : 1649.
Size : 39 × 62½ ins.
In the possession of the Trustees of the late Duke of Hamilton.

WILLIAM HAMILTON, 2ND DUKE OF HAMILTON

WHEN the younger son (1616-1651) of the second Marquis of Hamilton, after being educated at Glasgow University and spending a considerable time abroad, was introduced at Charles I.'s Court at the age of one-and-twenty, he became a great favourite. In 1639 he was created Earl of Lanark, and the following year he succeeded the poet Earl of Stirling as Secretary for Scotland, but exercised little influence, the real power being in his brother's hands. He shared in the Duke's downfall in 1643, but escaped to Scotland, where he joined the Covenanting party. Three years later he regained the King's confidence, and urged him to agree to the demands of the English Parliament. Failing in that, he became a chief party in the engagement to rescue Charles, and was active in the preparations for the Scottish incursion which ended in defeat at Preston. He then took refuge in Holland, whence, now Duke through his brother's execution, he returned to Scotland with Charles II. to take part in the campaign of 1651 and lose his life, after showing great courage, in the battle of Worcester.

JOHN MAITLAND, DUKE OF LAUDERDALE

GRAND-NEPHEW of William Maitland of Lethington, Queen Mary's Secretary, and eldest son of the first Earl of Lauderdale and his wife, a daughter of Lord Chancellor Seton, John Maitland (1616-1682) came of able

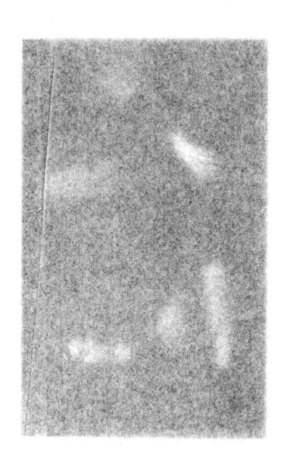

PLATE XXXVI

...LS OF HAMILTON A... D LAUDERDALE

...WILLIAM HAMP...ON, 2... D...KE OF ...MILTO

W...............................Duke of Hamilton ....Court at the ....Secretary ....Scotland, ...Court.............. These.................................Kings ....Duke of Lauderdale, ...party in the cause..............Prince Charles ....for the Scottish.................................and indeed ....Hamilton who, as...Duke, brought ....returned to Scotland with Charles...............part in the ....the battle...

...AITLAND, DUKE OF LAUDERDALE

...NEPHEW...William Maitland of Lethington, Queen Mary's ....and eldest son of the...Earl of Lauderdale and his wife, ...Lord Chancellor Schaw-Jean Maitland...

DUKES OF HAMILTON AND LAUDERDALE

stock on both sides. Little is known of his early life, but by 1648 he had shown such zeal in the Presbyterian cause that he was appointed a commissioner fof the Solemn League and Covenant and a delegate to the Westminster Assembly of Divines. Yet during the negotiations for Charles I.'s surrender at the close of the Civil War he passed secretly to the King's side, and in 1647 he was a principal in the 'Engagement,' but was not present when the Scots were defeated at Preston in the following year. He conveyed the invitation of the Committee of Estates to Prince Charles and accompanied him to Scotland, where, however, he was still regarded with suspicion by the extreme Covenanters; and, taken prisoner by Cromwell at Worcester, he was not liberated until the Restoration, when he was appointed Scottish Secretary. Middleton was High Commissioner, but Lauderdale's intimacy with the King gave him enormous influence, and in 1668 he ousted his rival and replaced him by Rothes, a tool of his own. Later, Rothes had to go also, and Lauderdale, ruling Scotland in his own unscrupulous fashion, made the Crown supreme in Church and State for a time, and his own name infamous for ever. Created a Duke and a Knight of the Garter in 1672 and made an English peer two years later, a member of the Cabal and sole arbiter in Scottish affairs, he was now at the height of his power; and although there were signs of opposition from the Scots nobility, and the English Parliament more than once addressed the King for his removal, he continued to hold office until after an apoplectic stroke in the spring of 1680, when he resigned. Two years later he died, but in the interval he had been deprived of all his offices. In the year he was made a Duke he married, as his second wife, the Countess of Dysart, a woman of strong will, who ruled him as he ruled Scotland, and there is no doubt that her ambition and her demands for money and for places for her friends contributed in no small degree to the scandal of her husband's administration.

OF the three principal portraits of this Duke of Hamilton, the earliest is the noble full-length by Daniel Mytens, lent to the Scottish National Portrait Gallery, which represents him as Earl of Lanark, and was painted before 1642, when the artist died. Other portraits of him by the same painter exist. The next, that reproduced, is dated 1649, and the third belongs to the following year, and is signed by Adrianc Hanneman. In all three the cast of countenance, although the features are not coarse, is morose and heavy, and his hair and eyes are dark brown; but while the moustache in the Mytens and the moustache and tuft in the Janssens are lighter than the hair, in the Hanneman,—of which versions exist at Windsor (the signed picture), Holyrood (where there are two, both titled 1st Duke), and Kinnaird Castle,—the moustache and tuft are as dark as the hair. Other portraits, including the print by R. White in Bishop Burnet's *Memoirs of the Hamiltons*, and specially the bust portraits in armour at Holyrood and Biel, show a more refined and sharp-cut face; but there is little doubt that the three described are the most reliable.

If there are a number of portraits of Hamilton, those of Lauderdale, who figures with him in the group by Janssens, are still more numerous, and, as could scarcely fail with a face so clearly marked, there is substantial agreement amongst them. He was a fair, reddish-haired, and gross-looking man, with a flabby face, heavy features, a slobbery mouth, and a double chin; but his expression was haughty, he bore himself proudly, and loved to be painted in his Court finery and orders. In this group, however, both he and Hamilton are dressed in black, with simple white collars and cuffs, evidently mourning for Charles I., who was executed in the year it was painted, and Lauderdale's face is not so heavy or so debased in type as in his later portraits. In those painted in his days of prosperity and power, such as the full-length at Thirlestane; the group of himself and the Duchess, which passed with other family pictures and possessions into the possession of the Dysart family through the lady; the three-quarter-lengths at Langton, Dalkeith and elsewhere, and other portraits, John Duke of Lauderdale appears in gorgeous raiment. Of the miniatures, that by Cooper (1609-1672) in the Royal collection at Windsor is probably the best, but those by Lawrence Crosse (1650?-1724) and Penelope Cleyn are interesting also.

It has been suggested that the group in question was formed by bringing two separate portraits together, but, while the canvas shows a vertical join between the figures, the design is too complete for that to be probable, and careful examination shows that Lauderdale's hand in the Hamilton half is not a later addition. This, combined with the fact that both the sitters were in Holland in 1649, and that the idea underlying the passing of the rolled-up paper from one to other seems to have some reference to the engagement for Charles I.'s rescue, in which they were the chief parties, makes it all but certain that it was painted as it now exists. There are two or three versions of the Hamilton half, but, so far as is known, none of the Lauderdale.

PLATE XXXVII

DAVID LESLIE, 1ST LORD NEWARK

1610 ?–1682

Painter : Sir PETER LELY (1618-1680).
Size : 48 × 39 ins.
In the possession of the EARL OF ROSEBERY, K.G., K.T.

ENTERING the service of Gustavus Adolphus at an early age, David
Leslie, fifth son of Sir Patrick Leslie of Pitcairly, Fifeshire, had considerable experience of soldiering before he returned to Scotland to
fight the battles of the Covenant. He acted as major-general under ' Old Leslie '
in the Scottish campaigns in England, contributed greatly to the victory at
Marston Moor (2nd July 1644), and carried out other important movements.
In 1645, however, he was summoned home to check Montrose's conquering
career, which he did by a surprise attack at Philiphaugh, and, after the transference of the King to the English Parliament, he was employed in suppressing
rebellion in the north. He declined to be a party to the ' Engagement,' but
when Charles II. had taken the Covenant, he accepted command of the army
raised to repel Cromwell's invasion, and had almost succeeded, when the clergy
interfered and precipitated the battle of Dunbar. At Worcester, a few months
later, the Scots were defeated again, and Leslie was taken prisoner, which he
remained until the Restoration, when he was created Lord Newark and given
a pension.

CONSIDERABLE discrepancy exists amongst the portraits of Lord Newark.
Some represent him as a fairish man with bluish eyes, and some as a
rather swarthy one, with eyes and hair to match; some, and these usually the
former, give him a moustache and pointed beard, while in the others he has
only a slight moustache and an indication of a tuft on the under lip. In certain

93

cases, however, as with a fine portrait, inscribed 'General Leslie,' at Newbattle Abbey, which has borne both names, it is probable that the former type has been confused with the portraits of Lord Leven, but the prevalence of the fairer is certainly a good argument in its favour. On the other hand, Lord Rosebery's portrait, which declares for the dark type, has been long accepted as a true likeness of Newark, and when in the Hamilton collection it was engraved for Lodge as his portrait. At the same time it seems to represent a younger man than Newark could well have been at the time the clothes he wears were in fashion.

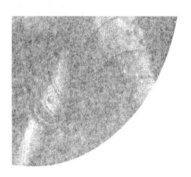

PLATE XXXVIII
GENERAL SIR THOMAS DALZELL

1599 ?–1685

Delineator : D. PATTON.
Engraver : P. VAN DER BANCK (1649-1697).
Size : 7⅛ × 5¼⅛ ins.
Reproduced from the rare contemporary engraving.

A SON of Thomas Dalzell of the Binns, West Lothian, where he was born, he entered the army at an early age, and is supposed to have seen foreign service at Rochelle, after which little is heard of him until he received a command in Monro's expedition (1642) to Ireland. He held Carrick-fergus for the King, and, when it capitulated, joined Charles II.'s army and was present at Worcester, where he was taken prisoner. But breaking from the Tower, he assisted in Middleton's rising in 1654 and then made his way to Russia and took service with the Czar Michaelovitch, in whose ferocious campaigns against Turks and Tartars Dalzell's naturally fierce nature was no doubt strengthened in its cruelty. He was recalled by Charles II. in 1666, and, made commander of the troops in Scotland, soon had an opportunity of displaying his peculiar talents at Rullion Green and in the suppression of the Westland Whigs, which followed. His rewards were a Privy Councillorship and the forfeited estates of the Mures of Caldwell; and from 1678 he sat in Parliament for his native county. In 1681 he raised the celebrated 'Scots Greys,' whose first work, of course, was dragooning the Covenanters. Yet this fierce old man was probably actuated by no other motives than a sense of discipline and an excessive and unquestioning loyalty, and latterly he devoted much time to laying out gardens and avenues and in cultivating flowers on his property at Binns

I F Dalzell's painted portraits are a bit of a puzzle, there is no doubt of the reliability of Van der Banck's engraving. Van der Banck was the General's contemporary, and whether Patton was the painter of the original, or only, as seems from the inscription on the plate more probable, the maker of a drawing, from an already existing portrait, for the engraver to work from, he was a contemporary also. Moreover, the *Memoirs of Captain Creichton*, one of the dragoons employed in hunting the Covenanters, contains a description of the 'Muscovite beast,' which in every point, except costume, confirms the print. 'Dalziel,' he writes, 'was bred up very hardy from his youth, both in diet and clothing. He never wore boots, nor above one coat, which was close to his body, with close sleeves, like those we call jockey-coats. He never wore a peruke, nor did he shave his beard since the murder of K. Charles I. In my time, his head was bald, which he covered only with a beaver hat, the brim of which was not above three inches broad. His beard was white and bushy, and yet reached down almost to his girdle. He usually went to London once or twice a year, and then only to kiss the King's hand, who had a great esteem for his worth and valour. His usual dress and figure when he was in London never failed to draw after him a great crowd of boys and young people, who constantly attended at his lodgings, and followed him with huzzas as he went to and from the Court. As he was a man of humour, he would always thank them for their civilities when he left them, and let them know exactly at what hour he intended to return.'

The print is rare, and one or two impressions seem to show a thin ring through the under lip; but that was surely too odd an ornament to escape Creichton and other chroniclers, and, as mention of it has not been found, it may be set down as a blemish or a later addition. A picture in the possession of a branch of the Dalzell family resembles the print closely, and is said to be the original. In it the eyes are dark grey, and the hair, beard, and moustache are white.

A three-quarter-length at Binns shows him standing, in armour, holding a baton, and a very similar picture, attributed to Riley, and supposed to have been painted about 1675 for the Duke of Rothes, is at Leslie House. But, contrary to the traditional vow, his face is clean shaven. From this it has been argued that these portraits were painted before 1649, but the man represented is considerably older than fifty, and it is probable that after the Restoration Dalzell may have felt relieved from his vow and at liberty to shave. In that case, however, one has to account for the discrepancy between the pictures and Creichton's specific statement.

96

IN
OUS?

Wolfson
Estates
Highland
would be a
Government

PLATE XXXIX

JOHN GRAHAM OF CLAVER-HOUSE, VISCOUNT DUNDEE

1643–1689

Painter and date : unknown.
Size : 28¾ × 24¼ ins.
In the possession of Miss Leslie Melville.

CLAVERHOUSE served his apprenticeship to war as a cornet in the Guards of the Prince of Orange, whose life he is said to have saved at the battle of Seneff (1674), and, on his return in 1677, he was given command of a regiment of horse raised to coerce the Covenanters of the South and West. He proved an able and unrelenting officer, but first comes into prominence in 1679, when he was defeated at Drumclog by the Whigs, whom persecution had driven to take up arms in their own and their religion's defence. Three weeks later he had his revenge at Bothwell Bridge for this affront to his master and himself, and the Government followed it up by even severer measures than before. His zeal and cruelty in the work of repression made him the most notorious of the persecutors, and fear and hatred built fables of a pact with the devil about him and his famous black charger. The hunted people dubbed him ' Bloody Clavers,' and the significance of that epithet still blights his memory.

Just before the Revolution Graham was created Viscount Dundee, and urged the King to meet William of Orange in arms ; and, when James fled, he attended the Convention of the Estates in Edinburgh, and, finding it against his master, rode north to raise the Highland clans. Possessed of somewhat similar qualities as a leader to Montrose, he soon had a following of some thousands, and, after several skirmishes, engaged the Government forces at Killiecrankie. The battle was short and decisive, Mackay's army was cut to pieces, the victory was brilliant and complete ; but Dundee was mortally wounded, and without him the Jacobite cause was hopeless in Scotland and the Revolution complete.

SCOTTISH PORTRAITS

THE principal portraits of Claverhouse number three, two paintings and one engraving, and the latter is probably a variation of one of the former. That reproduced is supposed to have been painted in Holland, when the sitter was a cornet in the Dutch Guards, and is one of the most charming portraits of its period. With rich, dark brown, flowing locks, and dark grey eyes, rosy complexion and soft, delicate features, his beauty is almost feminine, and seems to belie the cruelty inalienably associated with his name. Looking at it, one understands why the 'Bloody Clavers' became the 'Bonnie Dundee' of Sir Walter Scott's song. It is on this portrait that the excessively rare mezzotint by R. Williams (*fl.* 1690) seems to be founded, for, except that the position is reverse, the features heavier and the expression older, it is similar. In an old picture (29½ × 24½ ins.) in the possession of the Grahams of Airth, the face, although less beautiful and a little older, is not unlike the Melville in type and features, and has dark hair and dark blue eyes; but the head, lit in a similar way, is farther turned to the left, and the shoulders, over which the ends of the long wig stream, are shown in profile in that direction. The black and white miniature in the Scottish Portrait Gallery is rather prettier in face, but resembles the Airth picture in pose and arrangement. The second important original (48 × 89 ins.) is at Glamis, and represents Dundee in his maturity. He is shown three-quarter-length, wearing a buff coat and breastplate and carrying a baton, and has dark grey eyes and a brown wig. Attributed to Lely, it was painted, perhaps, in the summer of 1679, when he was in London, after Bothwell Bridge; but Mark Napier inclined to give it to Kneller, with the date 1688, when Graham became a Viscount. Not having seen this portrait, I can offer no opinion as to its authorship, but the absence of any symbol of his new honour is as good an argument against the later date as the presence of the leading staff is in its favour, while the state of turmoil on the eve of the Revolution makes it improbable that there was time for likeness-making. It is engraved in Lodge and in Napier's *Memoirs of Viscount Dundee*, in which prints of the Melville, Williams, and Airth portraits are also given. Other portraits, mostly versions of those already mentioned, are at Lochinch, Cultoquhey, Lee, Abbotsford, the Albert Institute, Dundee, and elsewhere, but those described are the most interesting. No contemporary description of his appearance is known, but his Highland followers called him 'Ian Dhu Cean'—Black John the Warrior.

98

SIR GEORGE MACKENZIE, BART

SIR

B

a ter the rsot
evil law. A lo
the Restoration, a
and his brillient
As member for
trong supporte
he was made King
Covenanters and o
zeualitie he cernd
God never lost a cere
fa of to of or a

PLATE XL
SIR GEORGE MACKENZIE OF ROSEHAUGH

1636–1691

Painter: Sir GODFREY KNELLER (1646-1723).
Size: 30 × 25 ins.
In the possession of the FACULTY OF ADVOCATES.

'**B**LOODY MACKENZIE,' for that was the name that his actions during the most important epoch of his career earned him, belonged to the Seaforth branch of the clan. He was born in Dundee, and, after the usual course at St. Andrews and Aberdeen, went to Bourges to study civil law. Admitted advocate in 1659, he was readmitted immediately after the Restoration, and, in spite of his early sympathies with the national party and his brilliant defence of the Marquis of Argyll, rose rapidly in his profession. As member for Ross-shire, he opposed Lauderdale, but in 1674 he became a strong supporter of the Government and was knighted, while three years later he was made King's Advocate. Mackenzie now had the prosecution of the Covenanters and other crown prisoners in his hands, and, while observing legal formalities, he carried his task out ruthlessly. One of his boasts was that he had never lost a case for the King, and to attain that end he did not scruple to strain the law or use torture. At the Revolution, after attending the Convention and voting against the resolution which deprived James of the crown, he withdrew to England, where he died. Yet, like Dalzell—'the Muscovite beast'—who cultivated flowers, he had a tenderer side to his nature, and interest in books and learning is the redeeming feature in his career. It was on a proposal of his, when Dean of Faculty, that the Advocates' Library was founded, and he delivered a Latin oration at its inauguration. He was the author of many books, 'some of law, and all full of faults; for he was a slight and superficial man.'

SCOTTISH PORTRAITS

AS is appropriate, an excellent portrait of Mackenzie hangs in the Parliament House, with which his name is doubly associated, through his legal career and his relation to the Advocates' Library. This, or another version, for several good ones exist, was well engraved in 1686, during Mackenzie's life, by R. White, and the large and strong but rather coarse features, the heavy eyebrows, prominent nose, and large snarling mouth, indicate clearly what manner of man he was—ambitious and able, but without scruples or mercy. His complexion is sallow, his long wig matches his dark brown eyes and eyebrows, and he wears a purple cloak and a white lace scarf. The contemporary print by P. Van der Banck (1649-1697), of which the original is unknown, shows a fuller view of the face; but, while like the Lely in features, is much less subtle and convincing in expression.

PLATE XLI

SIR JAMES DALRYMPLE
Ist VISCOUNT STAIR

1619–1695

Painter: Sir John B. Medina (1659-1710).
Date: about 1690.
Size: 49 × 37 ins.
In the possession of the Earl of Stair, K.T.

ONLY child of the Laird of Stair, a small estate in Ayrshire, Dalrymple
was educated at Mauchline School and Glasgow College, where he
graduated in 1635. He then entered Glencairn's regiment, with
which he served until 1641, when he returned to teach logic and morals in his
Alma Mater. In 1648, however, he was admitted advocate, and, during the
two following years, acted as secretary to the commissions sent to Holland to
invite Charles II. to Scotland. A period of practice at the bar followed, but
in 1657, on Monk's recommendation, Cromwell raised him to the bench. Confirmed in this position at the Restoration, he resigned rather than submit to
interference with his judicial independence, but was reinstated by the King, and
in 1679 became President of the Court of Session. He did not approve the
strong measures taken against the Covenanters, and when the Test Act was
passed, strove to mitigate its severity, was deprived of office, and took refuge
in Holland. His *Institutions of the Laws of Scotland*, which has been described
as the greatest work on that subject, had appeared in 1681, and he devoted his
exile to preparing a 'breveat' of decisions of the Court of Session, and to writing
a philosophical treatise.

Dalrymple returned on board the ship which brought William of Orange
to England, and soon he was reappointed President of the Session, and made a
peer, with the title Viscount Stair. Yet his last years were clouded by private
sorrows and public calumny. Lady Stair, whose part in raising the family

101

fortunes had been great, and who was accused of trafficking in the black arts, died in 1692, and the connection of his son, the Master of Stair, with the massacre of Glencoe was used as a lever against him by his enemies. Yet amongst his contemporaries he stands out as a just judge and a man of integrity as well as a great lawyer. Sir George Mackenzie, who knew him well, says, 'Really Stair was a gentleman of excellent parts, of an equal wit and universal learning; but most considerable for being so free from passions, that most men thought this equality of spirit a mere hypocrisy in him. This meekness fitted him extremely to be a President. . . . But that which I admired most in him was, that in ten years' intimacy I never heard him speak unkindly of those who had injured him.'

LORD STAIR has two portraits of the founder of his house, and the bust size (80 × 25 ins.) is probably a replica of that reproduced. Both are attributed to Medina, and at New Hailes, in the possession of a branch of the Dalrymple family, there is an excellent version of the smaller, which has a completer history and may be the original of the others. They show him in a red and ermine robe, with gold lace above the lower fur bands, which is not legal and is probably a peer's treated with some little artistic licence, and the original was probably painted immediately after he was made a viscount, and shortly after Medina arrived in Scotland. His was a very clearly marked type of face, and traces of it are still found in his descendants. A copy of the three-quarter-length at Oxenfoord was presented by the present Earl to the Parliament House, Edinburgh; and Sir Walter Dalrymple of North Berwick owns a portrait by Scougall in which the Lord President is shown wearing legal robes.

taken to Italy by S.Bt of N.Berwick, and has now been lost.

THE LANGHAM STREET PORTRAIT

PLATE XLII

SIR JOHN DALRYMPLE
1ST EARL OF STAIR

1648-1707

Painter and date: unknown.
Date: probably 1688.
Size: 50 × 40 ins.
In the possession of the EARL OF STAIR, K.T.

LORD PRESIDENT STAIR'S eldest son was educated for the law, and early gained a reputation for ability and eloquence, but, on his father's flight to Holland, he was imprisoned and, for opposing Claverhouse, deprived of his office of hereditary bailie of Glenluce. In 1686, however, he made his peace with James's Government and was appointed King's Advocate, but reluctance to prosecute those who attended conventicles led to his being degraded to the office of Justice-Clerk. At the Revolution he declared for William and Mary, to whose designs he had been privy, and was one of those sent to London to offer them the crown. The elder Dalrymple was now reappointed Lord President, and created Viscount Stair; the younger became Lord Advocate and chief official adviser on Scottish affairs, and, despite great opposition, did much to ensure a satisfactory settlement. But the Master's policy was sullied by the massacre of Glencoe, an act of treachery which in result drove him from public life, and left a lasting stigma on his name. In 1695 the old lord died, but it was not until five years later that his son took his seat in Parliament, and he never held office again. Yet he continued to exercise considerable influence, and the carrying of the Act of Union was due very largely to his tact, skill, and eloquence. The strain of these stormy debates wore him out, however, and he died suddenly on 8th January 1707. He had been created an Earl four years before.

THE principal portrait of the first Earl, owned by his family, is a three-quarter-length by an unknown painter. He has greyish-blue eyes and dark eyebrows, and is represented wearing a robe of scarlet, with white

103

hood and edgings, which closely resembles that to be seen in contemporary portraits of Judges of the King's Bench in England, and is not unlike that associated at that time with the office of Lord Justice-Clerk, which he held for a brief period. If from this, one may surmise that the portrait shows Stair as Justice-Clerk, and the apparent age of the subject confirms the supposition, it was probably painted in 1688. An oval (29½ × 24½ ins.), in the same possession and attributed to Medina, shows a more animated, and perhaps a more refined face, with grey-blue eyes and darkish-grey eyebrows. While the wide-nostrilled nose is slightly *retroussé* in this rendering, the curved and medium-sized mouth, the double chin and rounded contours appear in both. The Medina three-quarter-length in armour at New Hailes is less interesting.

JOHN HAMILTON 2ND LORD BELHAVEN

PLATE XLIII

JOHN HAMILTON, 2ND LORD BELHAVEN

1656-1708

Painter and date: unknown.
Size: 29½ × 24 ins.
In the possession of Mrs. HAMILTON OGILVY.

ELDEST son of Robert Hamilton, Lord Presmennan, judge of the Court of Session, John Hamilton succeeded his wife's grandfather, the first Lord Belhaven, by special remainder in 1679, and two years later made himself conspicuous by opposing the Government and was imprisoned. A staunch Protestant, he worked for the settlement of the crown on William and Mary, and commanded the Haddingtonshire troop of horse at Killiecrankie (1689). He was one of the strongest supporters and largest subscribers to the Darien scheme, which turned out so disastrously for Scotland, and he wrought for the improvement of agriculture at home. But it was during Queen Anne's reign that Belhaven bulked most largely in public affairs. He had been a strong advocate of the Act of Security, and, when parliamentary union was proposed, he became its most eloquent opponent. His speech against it is perhaps the most famous in the annals of the Scots Parliament, and is said to be the only specimen of Scots oratory that has found a place in collections of English rhetoric. This impassioned opposition led to imprisonment, and in 1708 he was taken to London on suspicion of favouring the Pretender, and, being released on bail, died a few days later.

THIS, the family portrait of Lord Belhaven, needs no description, for it is in complete agreement with what is known of his appearance. A contemporary speaks of him as of 'a good stature, well set, of a healthy constitution, black complexion, and graceful manly presence,' and the words are echoed by the picture.

PLATE XLIV

SIR WILLIAM BRUCE, BART., OF KINROSS

Died 1710

Painter: John Michael Wright (1625 ?-1700).
Date: 1665.
Size: 28¾ × 24½ ins.
In the possession of Sir Charles Bruce, K.C.M.G.

THE date of his birth is uncertain, but, while still young, he played a considerable part in the Restoration, having been sent, it is said, by General Monk to the young King to acquaint him with his intentions. In the very year of the King's return he was appointed Clerk of Bills, eight years later he was made a baronet, and in 1681 he became the representative of Kinross-shire in Parliament. But it is as an architect that he claims a place among famous Scots. Appointed 'King's surveyor and master of works' in 1671, he is best remembered as the designer of Holyrood as it now is; of Harden, Lord Polwarth's house on Borthwick Water; of Kinross on his own estate; and of Hopetoun as it was before William Adam altered it and added the wings.

ALTHOUGH Wright was a Scotsman, few portraits by him are to be found in his own country, but amongst them this of Sir William Bruce is perhaps the best. Painted when Bruce, to judge from the picture, was about thirty years of age, it represents him as a handsome young man with long brown-black curly hair and dark grey eyes. He wears an embroidered white muslin scarf and a pink-purple and yellow striped dressing-gown-like garment, and holds a port-crayon, emblematic of his artistic pursuits. The picture is signed and dated, and as Wright had gone to London many years before, and was a rival of Lely in 1665, it must have been painted there. It has been attributed to Medina, and described as one of his finest works; but not only the

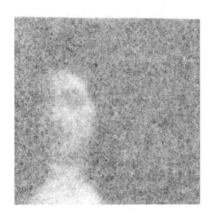

PLATE XLIV

WILLIAM BRUCE, BART., OF KINROSS

SIR WILLIAM BRUCE BART.
D. 17..
BUSSELL EXHIBITION GALLERY

SIR WILLIAM BRUCE, BART., OF KINROSS

signature, and date, but the style and refinement of the result, make that impossible. An indian-ink drawing (6½ × 5½ ins.) in the Scottish National Portrait Gallery depicts him as an older man with a face more marked in character and slightly fuller in contour, but substantially the same in type and feature. It looks like a drawing for engraving purposes; but prints are unknown, and the location of the original—if there is one—has not been ascertained.

PLATE XLV

JAMES DOUGLAS, 4TH DUKE OF HAMILTON

1658-1712

Painter: Sir John B. Medina (1659-1710).
Date: 1708.
Size: 49 × 40 ins.
In the possession of the Royal College of Surgeons, Edinburgh.

WILLIAM, second Duke of Hamilton, having left no direct heir, the titles devolved upon Anne, eldest daughter of the first Duke, who married Lord William Douglas, son of the first Marquis of Douglas. Their son, subsequently fourth Duke, was educated at Glasgow University and abroad, and as Earl of Arran occupied a prominent position at the Court of James II. and VII., whose falling fortunes he, at one time, seemed likely to support. He ended, however, in acquiescing in the new order of things, and in 1698 his mother resigned the family honours in his favour. The Darien scheme obtained his support, and he opposed parliamentary union until the last moment, when he threw obstacles in the way of the opposition; but he continued to be regarded as favourable to the exiled house, and his appointment in 1712 as ambassador extraordinary to France was regarded by the Jacobites as a happy augury of Queen Anne's intentions. But in the midst of magnificent preparations for his departure, he was killed, not without strong suspicions of treachery, in a duel forced upon him by Lord Mohun.

Except his father, who was created Duke for life, he was the first Douglas Duke of Hamilton, but he seems to have inherited the vacillatory nature of the Hamiltons. In the pages of *Esmond* he makes an heroic figure as the hope of the Jacobites, but in reality, though not wanting in personal courage, he lived in a state of chronic indecision, and was always ill when definite political action became necessary.

108

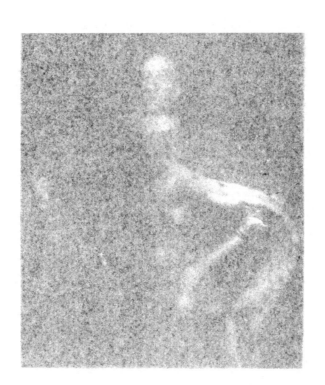

PLATE XLV

...ES DOUGLAS, ... DUKE
OF HAMILT...

...

WILLIAM, second Duke ... Hamilton, ... the ... direct heir, the ... of ... daughter of the first Duke, ... married L... Douglas, son of the last Marquis of ... The ... his ... Duke was educated at Glasgow University, and about ... earl of America ... a prominent position in the ... of James ... this ... and ... at one time seemed ... to support. He ... became ... opposer ... the new order of things, ... 1718 also ... and the ... by reasons to be ... The Peace of ... Conserved ... appealed ... he opposed pacification until the ... the Peace ... and the ... of the opposition; but ... he ... to be regarded as favorite ... of the ... of James, and his ... title as ... the ... treaty ... Peace was regarded ... a happy course of the ... his ... reasons. But in ... magnificent preparations for his departure ... was killed, and ... upon ... in a duel ... upon him by Lord

... was created Duke ... he ... was the first Douglas of ... but he seems to have inherited the warlike nature of ... in the pages of ... and he makes so inside figure as the ... the ... both valiantly, though not ... in personal courage, by Rod ... over ... on ... and was always ill when definite personal action seem ... necessary.

JAMES I ... EAP 4th DUKE OF HAMILTON
...
PAINTED BY SIR ... MEDINA

JAMES DOUGLAS, 4TH DUKE OF HAMILTON

A BUST portrait (29 × 24¼ ins.) by Kneller, of which several versions exist, depicts Thackeray's Duke as a handsome youth with an open and expressive countenance, dark yellowish-grey eyes, and long dark ringlets. One of these belongs to the family, as do an oval-bust in armour at Holyrood, and an imposing and martial-like full-length (98½ × 57½ ins.), lent to the Scottish National Portrait Gallery; but as the latter is signed 'G. Kneller, Baronet' (which places it at least three years after Hamilton's death), one hesitates to accept it as strictly contemporary, and inclines to regard it as a posthumous creation intended to take its place amongst the other full-lengths at Hamilton, where there is no other portrait of him on this scale. To this it may be objected that, as he wears the ribbon and badge of the Thistle, and not of the greater honour of the Garter, it was probably painted before 1712, when he received the latter order, which, however, he only held three weeks. No such doubt troubles one in connection with the three-quarter-length in the Surgeons' Hall, for it is one of many portraits painted by Medina for the Society to which it still belongs, and the painter predeceased his sitter. The Duke was elected an honorary fellow of the College of Surgeons on July 4, 1700, and the portrait reproduced is signed 'Jo. Medina Fecit 1703' in the left lower corner. For many years it has borne the name of Sir William Hamilton, Lord Whitelaw, and is so catalogued in the list of the Society's portraits; but the fact that the personage represented wears the order of the Thistle, while that in the College portrait by the same artist, which at present bears the Duke's name, wears the robes of Lord Justice-Clerk, to which Whitelaw was appointed a year after the Duke's portrait was painted, added to the proof of likeness, puts the question of who's who beyond dispute. As it was shown with its proper title in the 1867 Exhibition of National Portraits, the name-plates must have been transposed since then, and the error so originated has been perpetuated until now. In Medina's portrait Hamilton is scarcely so distinguished and good-looking as in Kneller's renderings, but in it one probably comes closer to the real man. 'He is of middle stature, well made, of a black complexion, a brisk look,' says Macky, and amongst his portraits that reproduced seems nearest the verbal description, the 'brisk look' specially not being very apparent in Lely's handsomer portraits.

PLATE XLVI
REV. WILLIAM CARSTARES
1649–1715

Painter: WILLIAM AIKMAN (1682-1731).
Date: 1710-15.
Size: 49½ × 39 ins.
In the possession of the UNIVERSITY OF EDINBURGH.

BORN in his father's manse at Cathcart, near Glasgow, he was educated at the University of which he was to become Principal, and at Utrecht, where so many Scots studied and sheltered during the Troubles, and where he met the Prince of Orange, under whose auspices he was to play so important a part. Having returned to England, his strong Presbyterian sympathies led to suspicion and arrest, and although he was never brought to trial, it was five years before he was released. In 1683 he was arrested again, for supposed complicity in the Rye-House Plot, and sent to Edinburgh, so that he might be forced to confess through torture. By 1686-7 Carstares was back in Holland and chaplain to the Prince, whom he accompanied to England at the Revolution. He was now deep in William's confidence, and his advice on all Scottish affairs was so constantly asked and acted upon that he was nicknamed the Cardinal by the Jacobites. His statesmanship contributed in no small degree to the success of the Revolution settlement, and to securing the Hanoverian succession, while his influence in favour of the Union of 1707 was of the greatest moment. In 1703, after King William's death, he had been made Principal of Edinburgh University, for the advancement of which he did much, and, having been appointed minister of Greyfriars, he was no less than four times Moderator of the Assembly, in which he exercised great power.

EDINBURGH University possesses an excellent portrait of its most famous Principal, by Aikman, and, if one presumes, as is more than probable, that it was painted after the artist's return from Italy, it represents him as he was

110

PLATE XLVI

WILLIAM CARSTARES

REV. WILLIAM CARSTARES

between 1710 and his death, five years later. A fresh-complexioned and fat-faced old man, with small and clear blue-grey eyes, under low and slightly arched eyebrows, a somewhat snub and wide-nostrilled nose, a mouth with full and rather pouting lips, and a double chin, he sits, gowned in black with white bands, in an arm-chair, turning from a great open volume, which he steadies on a red-covered table, to look at the spectator. It seems the original of two or three replicas or old copies, and it was engraved badly by R. Cooper (1705-1764), and prints sold by 'Gavin Hamilton, bookseller, opposite to the Parliament Close, Edin'.'

PLATE XLVII

ANDREW FLETCHER OF SALTOUN

1655–1716

Painter: uncertain.
Size: 30 × 25 ins.
In the possession of the Earl of Stair, K.T.

SON and heir of Sir Robert Fletcher of Saltoun, he was educated by Gilbert Burnet, afterwards Bishop of Salisbury, whom his father had induced to accept the parish, but, while he benefited by Burnet's instruction, he did not imbibe his political principles and became an ardent Republican. His father had died in 1664, and at the age of twenty-three he sat in Parliament for his own county, East Lothian, and supported the opposition to Lauderdale. For this and other reasons Fletcher was treated as a malcontent, but that did not prevent his opposing the measures, and especially the Test, introduced by Lauderdale's successor, the Catholic Duke of York. About 1682 he sought refuge abroad, whence, after trying to persuade Monmouth to abandon his expedition, he accompanied him to England, where, however, a hasty action made it necessary for them to part, and Fletcher went to Spain, after which his movements are uncertain until 1688, when he joined William of Orange at the Hague, and returned home. Once more in Scotland, he became prominent in the patriotic party, which was striving to conserve Scottish interests, and an advocate of the Darien scheme. In 1708 he again entered Parliament, sitting for his old constituency, and took a leading part in trying to secure greater independence for Scotland in her relations with England, but with little success, for parliamentary union had become inevitable, and in 1707 it was carried. Next year Fletcher and Lord Belhaven, the other great opponent of union, with certain Jacobite suspects, were taken to London on suspicion, but they were soon released. His last years seem to have been spent in attempts to improve methods of agriculture in Scotland.

112

ANDREW FLETCHER OF SALTOUN

ANDREW FLETCHER OF SALTOUN

ANDREW FLETCHER OF SALTOUN

Before he retired into private life he published numerous trenchant pamphlets and speeches on public affairs, including the *Right Regulation of Government for the Common Good of Mankind* (1708), in which occurs the famous phrase, 'If a man were permitted to make all the ballads, he need not care who should make the laws of a nation.' Fletcher's contemporaries of all shades of opinion united in acknowledging the purity of his motives, the depth and sincerity of his convictions, and the disinterestedness of all his actions; and the word 'Patriot' exactly mirrors the estimation in which his memory is held by his countrymen.

SEVERAL portraits of Fletcher exist, but in every case they seem to have been derived from that in Lord Stair's collection at Oxenford. When first mentioned (1790), it belonged to Sir John Dalrymple of Cranston, from whose family it passed to that of its present owner; and it appears from the letter written at that time to Lord Buchan, who was anxious to secure a likeness of Fletcher, that the Saltoun people themselves had only a copy of the Cranston or Stair portrait.

LIEUTENANT-GENERAL HENRY FLETCHER TO THE EARL OF BUCHAN.

'SALTON HALL, *29th April* 1790.

'MY DEAR LORD,—Your letter of the 81 Jany. last I had the honour to receive, and in consequence thereof took in with me all that we have, for Ancient Andrew which my Brother M.-Genl. Campbell took from one at Sir John Dalrymple's at Cranston and presented it to my late brother Andrew. But, my Lord, wee have a strong proof that the said picture (now with Miss Forbes) is a strong resemblance of our illustrious G⁴ Uncle. Lord Martiall, when last in Scotland being at Cranston (of himself), upon seeing the said picture said—"That is my worthy Friend Andrew Fletcher of Salton."'

Later, Lord Buchan, through his usual looseness of statement, gave the impression that the copy then made for him by Miss Anne Forbes, a niece of Aikman, to whom the Stair picture has been attributed, was an original, and it was engraved as such for Pinkerton, to whom his lordship sent a drawing—now in the Scottish National Portrait Gallery—for the engraver to work from. It is worth while, perhaps, to quote the inscriptions which Buchan wrote on this drawing, for they are at once characteristic of his enthusiasm and of the conditions under which Pinkerton's portrait-books were carried out. 'This is Fletcher of Saltoun concerning whom i have written. "This is Fletcher my countryman, the last of the Scots, whose religion was a Divine Philosophy of the Soul, and who set Marcus Brutus for his Pattern,"' is one, and the other is this footnote: ' N.B.—I have left the Periwig unfinished, and refer the Engraver to Sir Godfrey Kneller and the "Times"—I content myself with the Soul of Fletcher.' The drawing is dated, ' Dryburgh Abbey, December 18, 1794.' and marked ' For Mr. Pinkerton's *Iconographia Scotica.*'

As our reproduction speaks for itself as regards Fletcher's features and general air, it would serve no purpose to do more than note that he has dark bluish eyes, and wears a neutral brown wig, and a red and blue robe arranged in conventional folds. But the picture may be supplemented by Macky's description of him as ' a low thin man, brown complexion, full of fire, with a stern sour look,' and this evidence given concerning him in 1686, ' a little man with a brown periwig, of lean face pock-marked.'

PLATE XLVIII

SIR EWEN CAMERON
OF LOCHIEL

1629-1719

Painter and date: unknown.
In possession of DONALD CAMERON, Esq., of Lochiel.

IT is a greater distinction to be head of Clan Cameron than to represent a city in Parliament or to be a peer, even a Duke, for there are many of these, but only one 'Lochiel.' In the long succession in this famous chieftainship there are many noted names, but none more famous and honoured than that of Sir Ewen or Evan, the seventeenth of his line. This 'Ulysses of the Highlands,' as Macaulay dubbed him, was born in 1629, and, his father having died, he was brought up by the Marquis of Argyll. While still in Argyll's keeping a stolen interview with Sir Robert Spottiswood (1596-1646) embued the young chief with Royalist principles, and in 1652 he called out his clan to join the Earl of Glencairn in his attempt in favour of Charles II. Lochiel continued in arms after Glencairn submitted to Cromwell, and a military station was established at Inverlochy specially to hold him in check; but it was not until Monk offered to receive his submission without requiring him to disown the King that Cameron came in. He accompanied Monk to London at the Restoration, when he received no particular mark of favour, but in 1681 he was knighted. It was in Lochaber that the clans gathered in 1690, and Lochiel's advice decided Dundee to give battle at Killiecrankie, where the charge of the Camerons, led by Sir Evan, did much to win the day. When the Jacobite standard was unfurled on the braes of Mar in 1715, Lochiel was too old to take the field in person, but his interest in the old cause was keen as ever, and he sent his son and clansmen. His career was distinguished by many acts of personal bravery and daring, yet he was never wounded by an enemy, and even in his ninetieth year his eyes retained their vivacity, and he had not lost a single tooth.

SCOTTISH PORTRAITS

He was tall, finely proportioned, and an adept in war and the chase, and the Gaelic epithet 'Evan Dhu,' that is Black Evan, by which he was known, referred to his swarthy complexion and very dark brown hair.

AS it is difficult to see what chances Lochiel had of being painted at home, it is possible that this, 'the only original portrait of Sir Ewen now extant' [*Memoirs of Sir Ewen Cameron* (1842)], was painted in London in 1660, or in Edinburgh in 1681. He was fifty-two at the latter date, and if the picture suggests a younger man, Lochiel was more than usually active, and had killed what is said to have been the last wolf in Scotland during the previous year. But the itinerant portrait-painter was ubiquitous, and there are portraits of other Highland gentlemen of this period which show considerable resemblance in handling and general type to the picture in question, which was engraved many years ago with these lines inscribed beneath it:—

> 'The Honest Man, whom Virtue sways,
> His God adores, His King obeys;
> Does factions, Men's rebellious pride
> And threatening Tyrants' rage deride;
> Honour's his Wealth, his Rule, his Aime
> Unshaken, fixt, and still the same.'

The plate has no date or engraver's name, and impressions are very rare.

ILL[...]

BROUGH[...]
seve[...]
s sald[...]
Bahamas [...]
with the [...]
conceive [...]
le [...]
[...]
I ou[...]
in 160[...]
Government [...]
but, as his [...]
Edward's [...]
which he now [...]
opportunity [...]
South of tradi[...]
account of the [...]
and Sout[...] conce[...]
[...] The peace [...]
[...] acros[...] for [...]
[...] Ber[...]
[...]
[...]
[...]

PLATE XLIX
WILLIAM PATERSON
1658–1719

Draughtsman and date: unknown.
Reproduced same size as original.
In the BRITISH MUSEUM.

BROUGHT up on the farm where he was born, Paterson was about
seventeen when he left Dumfriesshire to find his way, as a pedlar it
is said, first to England and then to America. For some time he lived
in the Bahamas, where he acted in the capacity of a preacher, and, coming into
contact with the buccaneers from whom he learned much about trade in Central
America, conceived the design of a great trading colony at Panama. Returning
to Europe, he tried to have his plan taken up by the English Government, and
then, also unsuccessfully, in Hamburg, Amsterdam, and Berlin. He settled in
London as a merchant, and having made a considerable fortune in a short time, he,
in 1694, formulated a scheme for a national bank and succeeded in inducing the
Government to adopt it. He was an original director of this, the Bank of England,
but, as his co-directors objected to his activities in other directions, soon retired.
Paterson's next great project was a revival of the Darien one, in pursuance of
which he now removed to Edinburgh, where, as Scotland was anxiously waiting an
opportunity to expand its trade, it was taken up eagerly. 'The Company of
Scotland trading to Africa and the Indies' having been formed, the projector
accompanied the expedition when the first ships sailed in 1698. It was a great
and boldly conceived design, and but for unforeseen difficulties might have
succeeded. The point chosen for the trading-station was central, and Paterson's
idea of a canal across the Isthmus is even now being carried out. But it was
a tragic failure; disease and famine, external enmity and internal dissension,
combined to bring the great venture, in which Scotland had sunk all its available
capital, to a speedy close, and Paterson returned with all that were left of the
sanguine colonists. His health had suffered, but, having recruited, he engaged

in new projects, and amongst other things suggested improved methods for the control of the national finances. He contributed considerably to the success of the movement for parliamentary union, in which his keen intellect saw many advantages for his native land and the country as a whole, and he had a principal hand in drafting the trade and financial clauses of the Act of 1707.

ONLY one portrait of Paterson is known, and as it is a wash drawing, and reproduced full size, nothing can be said in comment except that it has been inserted in the British Museum copy of Paterson's *Two Treatises Relating to the Union* (b. 10408 f. 1 b.).

ANN,

P.
b.
S.
t.

ANN,

ANN, or Ann...
ta...
1691...
of her time, and... wa
She was but twelve... a...
illegitimate son, the D...
youthful couple Duke...
so dully with the Duke
faith Evelyn speaks of her...
Court Commoners...
...ed all those perso...
...y. By Monmouth...
...served many years...
...me and lost his...
...Charles third I and...
...y one.

Scott, Earl of Dalkei...
...rit to, daughter of...
...led a son Charl...

119

PLATE L

ANN, DUCHESS OF BUCCLEUCH AND SONS

Painter : Sir GODFREY KNELLER (1646-1723).
Date : about 1684.
Size : 88 × 60 ins.
In the possession of the DUKE OF BUCCLEUCH, K.G., K.T.

ANN, DUCHESS OF BUCCLEUCH

1651-1732

ANN, or Anna, as the name is sometimes given, third daughter of Francis, Earl of Buccleuch, succeeded her sister as Countess of Buccleuch in 1661. With an income of £10,000 a year, she was the greatest match of her time, and, while not yet in her teens, her hand was eagerly contested for. She was but twelve indeed when Charles II. married her to his and Lucy Walters' illegitimate son, the Duke of Monmouth, and he immediately created the very youthful couple Duke and Duchess of Buccleuch. A great favourite at Court, specially with the Duke of York, who tried to convert her to the Catholic faith, Evelyn speaks of her as 'one of the wisest and craftiest of her sex,' and in Count Grammont's opinion 'her person was full of charm and her mind possessed all those perfections in which the handsome Monmouth was so deficient.' By Monmouth she had several children, none of whom, except two sons, survived many years, and in 1685, when her husband made his bid for the throne and lost his head, the Duchess's conduct won admiration. She married Charles, third Lord Cornwallis, three years later, and lived to the great age of eighty-one.

JAMES SCOTT, Earl of Dalkeith (1674-1705), the eldest son, was married in 1693 to Henrietta, daughter of the first Earl of Rochester, and, dying before his mother, left a son who succeeded as second Duke of Buccleuch.

119

SCOTTISH PORTRAITS

HENRY SCOTT (1676-1730), the third but second surviving son of the Duchess, became a favourite with Queen Anne, who created him Earl of Deloraine and Viscount Hermitage in 1706, when he sat in the last Scottish Parliament and voted for union. He had a great reputation for courtesy, but his relations with his mother were none too cordial.

OF the portraits of Monmouth's Duchess, that reproduced is the most important. A life-size full-length, it represents her accompanied by her two sons. She wears a coronet, is gowned in white satin with lace sleeves, and holds a red velvet and ermine mantle; the elder boy wears a pale grey silk suit, and the younger a dark blue embroidered with white, and red stockings. It was engraved in mezzotint, 'Her Grace the Dutchess of Monmouth, ye Earle of Doncaster and ye Lord Henry. G. Kneller pinx.: sold by S. Beckett at the golden head in the Old Baily,' perhaps by J. Smith, whose name appears on the third state; but the date, 1688, usually assigned to the print, is improbable, and both picture and engraving were more probably executed a few years earlier. The designation, 'Dutchess of Monmouth,' would scarcely be used on a plate after her husband's execution; 'Earle of Doncaster' was a Monmouth and not a Buccleuch title, and lapsed in 1685; the lady does not wear the dress of a widow, which she was from 1685 to 1688, and the apparent ages of the boys in the picture—in the print both they and their mother look older—would be more suitable for 1685 or the preceding year. Next to this one may place the three-quarter-length (29¼ × 24¾ ins.), also at Dalkeith, which was attributed to Lely (1618-1680), when shown at the National Portrait Exhibition of 1868. This shows her seated, the figure turned slightly towards the right, and her hands lying in her lap, and the face, which is sweeter and more engaging in expression than in the Kneller, seems that of a woman of less than twenty-five. Here she wears a crimson dress, very low at the bosom, with white undersleeves. Other portraits are the ovals by Lely and Wissing, engraved in mezzotint by Lloyd and J. Beckett, and the half-length (49 × 38 ins.) by an unknown artist, at Dalkeith, in which a black page, carrying a bunch of grapes, attends his mistress.

EARL

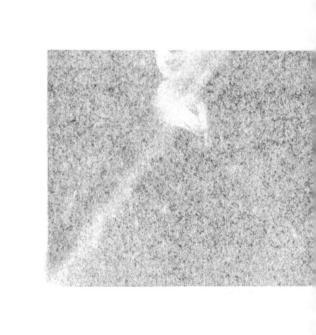

PLATE LI

JOHN ERSKINE, 11TH EARL OF MAR

1675–1732

Painter: Sir GODFREY KNELLER (1646–1723).
Date: about 1700?
In the possession of the EARL OF MAR AND KELLIE.

IF the part played by this Earl of Mar was quite out of proportion to his talents, it was of such a nature as to give his name enduring prominence in the history of Scotland. Son of the 10th Earl of the Erskine line, he was brought up as a supporter of the Revolution settlement, and acted as Scottish Secretary during the Union Parliament; but in 1710 he passed over to the new Tory ministers, Oxford and Bolingbroke, who found him employment as a Secretary of State, in which capacity he had much to do with Scottish affairs, specially in the North, where he had great personal influence. After the death of Queen Anne he made overtures to George I., but they were rebuffed, and the haughty Earl retired to Scotland, where, under the pretext of a great hunting, he brought together many powerful Highland chiefs and Jacobite gentlemen, and raised the standard of the Chevalier de St. George at Braemar. Soon he had a large following, and, although without military experience, assumed the chief command. He began with some small successes, and, having taken Perth, threatened the Lowlands; but he was undecided as a leader, and John, Duke of Argyll, commander-in-chief in Scotland, was enabled to make the most of the very inferior force at his disposal. Anticipating Mar's tardy movements, he forced battle at Sheriffmuir, near Dunblane, on the morning of Sunday, 13th November 1715. The left of each army was broken and put to flight, but, as Mar withdrew his men and abandoned his artillery, the fruits of victory were Argyll's. The rebel army was lying at Perth, shrinking from desertion, when the Chevalier arrived in Scotland, but he brought no troops, or arms, or

121

money, and his personality was not of a kind to inspirit desponding men. Mar now retreated northward before Argyll's advance, and, when the Prince, accompanied by the chief organiser of rebellion, slipped secretly on board ship at Montrose, and left his followers to shift for themselves, the '15 was virtually at an end. Mar acted as chief adviser to the Chevalier until 1724, when he lost his master's confidence through long-continued intrigues with the British Government, and the rest of his life was spent in retirement in Paris and Aix-la-Chapelle. Devoting his leisure to the study of architecture, he made some suggestions, such as the making of a canal between Forth and Clyde, and the building of the North and South Bridges in Edinburgh, which were carried out long afterwards.

THE most important portraits of the attainted Earl are in the possession of the Earl of Mar and Kellie at Alloa House. Three of them are by Kneller, and represent him before the Rebellion. The full-length in robes, in which he appears accompanied by his son, Thomas, Lord Erskine (1706-1766), for whom the estates were acquired after the '15, and which was reproduced in *The Earl of Mar's Legacies to Scotland and to his Son, Lord Erskine* (Scottish History Society, 1896), may, as the boy seems about seven years old, be dated approximately 1712-13. A three-quarter-length (let into the panelling of the billiard-room), which shows him as Governor of Stirling Castle, accoutred in armour and with a view of a castle in the background, is marked 'Kneller pinxit, 1709,' but may have been painted earlier, as the contemporary mezzotint, a bust with an armorial frame in line, by J. Smith, is clearly derived from it or a similar picture, and is dated 1703, and inscribed 'Ætatis suæ 28.' Still as this print exists in two states, the later of which is dated 1707, and shows the ribbon of the Thistle, which appears in the Alloa picture, but not in the earlier engravings, it may be a rather later version of a picture painted in 1703, or a little earlier. But whether 1703 be accepted as the date of this three-quarter-length or not, the portrait reproduced may be assigned to two or three years before the engraving, say to 1700, when he was five-and-twenty. In these portraits he is a haughty looking man of pale pinky complexion, with dark blue grey eyes and full red lips; and the full-length specially reminds one that Macky describes him as being fair complexioned and of low stature. He is well-favoured, but not stout, as he appears in the head and shoulders, front face, by Rigaud (1659-1743), and in the circular bust of him as an aged man, the

122

head seen in profile to the left, which represent him in later life in the present Earl's collection. Each of these gives him a double chin, and in the circular picture specially, his nose seems relatively more prominent than in earlier years.

If the engraving by P. Vandrebanc, after a drawing *ad vivum* by W. Hassell, which bears Lord Mar's name and arms, really represents him, it must be by that younger Vandrebanc, who is supposed to have followed his father's profession but of whose work nothing is known, for Pieter Vandrebanc died in 1697, when Mar was twenty-two, and the face in the print in question is that of a man of at least twice that age.

PLATE LII

JOHN CAMPBELL, DUKE OF ARGYLL AND GREENWICH

1678-1743

Painter: WILLIAM AIKMAN (1682-1731).
Size: 49 × 39 ins.
In the NATIONAL PORTRAIT GALLERY.
Photographic negative by Messrs. Walker and Cockerell.

ALTHOUGH the 10th Earl of Argyll was the first of the Campbells to attain the dignity of a dukedom, he contributed nothing to the lustre which his house had gained in the persons of his father, the Earl, who was beheaded in 1685, and his grandfather, who had suffered a similar fate at the Restoration. But his son, the second Duke, restored the prestige of the Argylls and acted a conspicuous part in the history of his country. His early years were spent in active service in King William's continental wars; but, on succeeding to the title in 1703, he turned for a while to civil affairs and acted as Commissioner to the Scots Parliament in 1705, when he secured the passing of the Act appointing commissioners to treat for parliamentary union, which, two years later, he advocated eloquently at the last meetings of the Estates. For these services he was given an English peerage as Earl of Greenwich, but, almost alone of the Scottish statesmen who supported the Union, he stood above popular suspicion of being influenced by personal or mercenary motives. Argyll then returned to the army and served with great distinction under Marlborough, of whose great reputation he seems, however, to have been jealous, until after Ramillies (1709), when he was given the chief command in Spain. But through want of support from the home Government he was able to accomplish little, and on his return he opposed the ministry and was deprived of his offices. His prompt action in the Privy Council when Queen Anne lay dying did much to secure the

124

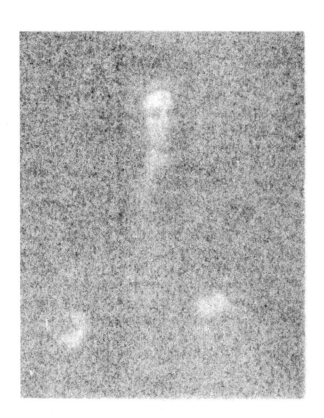

PLATE LII

... CAMPBELL, ... OF
... AND GRE... ...CH

1678-1743

...

...

...

The ... of Argyll was the first of the Campbells to ... a dukedom, he created ... long to the ... behaved in the person of his father, the ... and his grandfather ... I suffered a ... But his son, the second Duke, restored the ... and a conspicuous part in the history of his ... represent ... in the se... in King William's ... according to the d... in 1698, he ... for a ... as Commissioner to the S... Parliament in ... of the Act appointing commissioners to treat ... two years later, he advocated eloquently at the ... of the Union. For these services he was given an English ... but almost alone of the Scottish statesmen who ... in the settlement above suspicion of being influenced by ... Argyll then returned to the army and served ... Marlborough, of whose great reputation he seemed ... after Ramillies (1706), when he was ... a Scot. But though ... appear from the ... he was able to accomplish ... and on his return he ... and was deprived of his offices. His prompt action in the Privy Council when Queen Anne lay dying did much to assure th...

WILLIAM CHANCELLOR BRADSHAW
(1679-1747)
From the Bust of Chandos

JOHN CAMPBELL, DUKE OF ARGYLL

Hanoverian succession, and he was commander-in-chief in Scotland when the Earl of Mar held the great hunting at Aboyne and inaugurated the Rebellion of 1715. With a greatly inferior force—the armies were four thousand to twelve—he met the rebels at Sheriffmuir and defeated them, for, if the action itself was indecisive, he retained his ground, and the immediate results were those of victory. He followed up this success with measures which, without being unduly severe, extinguished rebellion, and, on going to London, was well received at Court; but before long he was deprived of all his appointments. By 1719, however, he was again in favour and was created Duke of Greenwich; but George II.'s accession (1727) and his own independent and somewhat touchy spirit once more deprived him of office, which, except for a brief period, he never again enjoyed. When, after the Porteous Mob in 1768, it was decided to penalise Edinburgh and to revoke the city charter, Argyll resented the proposal as an insult to Scotland, and was successful in his opposition. Pope's lines:

> 'Argyll, the state's whole thunder born to wield,
> And shake alike the senate and the field,'

express the regard in which he was held by his contemporaries; a noble monument by Roubiliac was erected to his memory in Westminster Abbey; and his character is vividly portrayed by Sir Walter Scott in *The Heart of Midlothian.*

DUKE JOHN was one of William Aikman's chief friends and patrons, and it is probable that the earliest portrait of him extant is the work of that painter. In 1785 Houbraken engraved a plate after an Aikman, in the possession of Sir Anthony Westcomb, Bart., the whereabouts of which is now unknown, but which, while differing from that in the London Portrait Gallery as regards costume, resembles it very closely in features and expression. These portraits must, of course, have been painted before 1731, but whether before or after 1723, when Aikman removed from Edinburgh to London on Argyll's advice, it is impossible to say. His face was one that retained its youth well, for there is little difference between it as rendered by Aikman and by Allan Ramsay, at least ten years later. Ramsay's imposing full-length at Inveraray, which shows him in his Garter robes, is dated 1740 on Faber's fine contemporary mezzotint, and must therefore be one of the earliest important portraits painted by the artist after his return from Italy to Edinburgh in the previous year. By both Aikman and Ramsay he is represented as a man of slight and graceful figure, with elegant hands and a head of smallish size. His unwrinkled forehead is rounded and broad rather than high, his eyebrows are high arched above large dark grey eyes, which, set widely apart over high cheek bones, look straight out of the picture; he has a low-bridged nose, slightly bulbous at the point; a medium-sized and well-shaped mouth, with full but not heavy lips; and a small, firm, and well-formed chin. As he wears a wig in both pictures, the colour of his hair cannot be stated. The engraving in Lodge (from a picture belonging to the Hon. G. A. Ellis at that time), which has been frequently repeated in other books, is quite different in type and cannot be accepted; but it is possible that the three-quarter-length at Dalkeith House represents him at an earlier age than the Aikmans. If of the Duke and by Kneller, to whom it is attributed, it must have been painted between 1710, when Argyll received the Garter, and 1723, when the artist died. In the excellent articles on certain Argyll portraits, contributed by Mr. J. H. Stevenson to the *Scottish Antiquary* in 1896-7, the Dalkeith picture was discussed and illustrated. Mr. Stevenson inclined to reject it as a portrait of the second Duke, but Lord Archibald Campbell, in a letter to the same journal, expressed a different opinion and stated that there was another version at Roseneath. As regards the full-length by Aikman in the Parliament House, which bears the name of Duke John, the articles referred to demonstrated conclusively that it represents not him but his brother, Archibald, third Duke of Argyll.

'Few of his years have a better understanding nor a more manly behaviour. He hath seen most of the Courts of Europe, is very handsome in appearance, fair complexioned, about twenty-five years old,' is Macky's description of him at the time he succeeded his father.

PLATE LIII

JOHN DALRYMPLE
2ND EARL OF STAIR

1673-1747

Painter: ALLAN RAMSAY (1713-1784).
Date: 1745.
Size: 43 × 39½ ins.
In the possession of the EARL OF STAIR, K.T.

THE third generation of the ennobled Dalrymples of Stair found in the second Earl a representative as illustrious in his own way as the Viscount and the first Earl had been in theirs. John Dalrymple was a second son, and having, when only eight years of age, shot his elder brother accidentally, his parents could not bear his presence, and he was sent to his grandfather, then in exile at Leyden, where he studied at the University. His early manhood was spent in King William's Flemish campaigns, but it was not until he joined the Duke of Marlborough as aide-de-camp in 1703 that he began to come to the front. He distinguished himself at the taking of Peer and Venloo, was present at Blenheim, and commanded a brigade at Ramillies. After Oudenarde, where he earned great praise, he was selected to carry the despatches to Queen Anne, and he was Major-General at Malplaquet; but in 1711 a change of ministry led to the recall of Marlborough, and Stair, who had succeeded his father four years before, went with him. Returning to Scotland, he became a leader in the Whig party; and, on the Hanoverian succession, he once more found employment, and was sent as Ambassador to Paris, where, by wonderful tact and diplomacy, he rendered invaluable services to the new *régime*, and added greatly to his reputation. In 1720, however, he was recalled, and, during Walpole's rule, divided his time between opposing the Government and introducing many successful improvements in agriculture on his estates. Walpole having been defeated in 1742, Stair was made a field-marshal and

127

given the command of the army sent to assist Austria; but after the victory at Dettingen, where George II. commanded in person, his plans were not acted upon, and he resigned. When in 1744 a Jacobite rising was anticipated, the old Marshal again offered his services to the King, and was appointed commander-in-chief of all the forces in South Britain. Two years later he died.

OF the two chief portraits of Lord Stair, the earlier is that by Kneller (1646-1728), of which the signed original is at Dumfries House, and of which versions exist at Douglas Castle (copy by Medina), Oxenfoord, in the possession of Mr. Scott of Gala, and elsewhere. Half-lengths, they show him as a handsome young man, with regular features, fair complexion, and dark blue eyes. He stands, the figure almost in profile to the left, holding a baton in his right hand and resting his left upon a table, upon which a small dog, with a collar lettered 'Earl of Stairs,' sits. The green ribbon of the Thistle crosses his dark armour, from under which the skirts of a long tunic hang. As Stair received the Thistle in 1710, and Kneller died in 1728, the picture was probably painted between these dates, most likely shortly after 1711, when Marlborough and he were recalled. It was engraved in mezzotint by R. Cooper (1715-1764), but impressions are excessively rare, only one being known to Chaloner Smith, and is apparently also the source of a line-engraving (an oval within an elaborate cartouche), which has no engraver's name or date, but which looks as if it might be contemporary. The other portrait, painted by Allan Ramsay in 1745, shows the Marshal near the close of his life, and is incomparably more characteristic. The face of the old diplomat and soldier dominates the picture, and is instinct with the many qualities which made him a remarkable man. He wears a scarlet coat and the ribbon of his order over a polished cuirass, and the figure is relieved and lost against a background of cloud and smoke. This picture was mezzotinted by J. Faber, a contemporary, probably just after Stair's death, for the plate is inscribed with all his titles and honours. Sir Charles Dalrymple has a fine replica at New Hailes. A bust in oils (20¾ × 16½ ins.) at Oxenfoord, and also attributed to Ramsay (a small version is in the Scottish National Portrait Gallery), belongs to about the same date. A profile, the prominent and straight-bridged nose continues the slope of the brow, and, the upper lip hanging slightly inwards, the under lip projects a little in front; the chin is firmly modelled, and the eye is not

128

LORD DALRYMPLE, 2ND EARL OF STAIR

deep set in the head. Here again he wears his orders on his armour. In a fourth picture ($48 \times 29\frac{1}{2}$ ins.) in the possession of his family, he is represented on horseback, and is accompanied by a black servant, who carries his helmet. Another and more important equestrian portrait belongs to Lord Cobham, who has a family interest in the picture, because Stair is accompanied by Colonel, afterwards Sir Richard Lyttleton, K.B. Like the Ramsay it belongs to his later years, and probably marks his last campaign.

PLATE LIV

SIMON FRASER, 12TH LORD LOVAT

1667-1747

Painter: WILLIAM HOGARTH (1697-1764).
Date: 1746.
Size: 25½ × 16½ ins.
In the NATIONAL PORTRAIT GALLERY.
Photographic negative by Messrs. Walker and Cockerell.

COMING of a Lowland family, which had established itself at Lovat on the river Beauly in the fourteenth century, Simon Fraser was educated at King's College, Aberdeen (M.A. 1688), where he acquired some knowledge and love of the classics, which clung to him to the very end of his remarkable career. He was cousin to the tenth Lord Lovat, with whom he so ingratiated himself that although that lord had a daughter, he bequeathed the estates to Simon. To unite his somewhat shaky claims with those of this lady, he decided to marry her, but when he captured Castle Downie, the daughter had fled, and in most brutal fashion he forced marriage upon the widow, a sister of the Marquis of Atholl. Outlawed for this and the accompanying acts, Fraser fled to France, where he associated with the Jacobites; but in 1700 he succeeded in playing Argyll off against Atholl, and secured a pardon. In 1702 he was again at St. Germains, engaged in intrigues with Louis XIV. and the Chevalier and his exiled supporters, who, however, suspected his integrity, and with justice, for, going to England, he betrayed them to the Duke of Queensberry. Having the audacity to return to France, he was thrown into the Bastille, from which he only obtained release by entering the Jesuit College at St. Omer. Stormy petrel that he was, the Rebellion of 1715 brought him to Scotland; and the husband of the Lovat heiress having declared for the Chevalier, Simon, as male-heir, recalled the clan from Mar's camp at Perth, and, being obeyed, aided Forbes of Culloden in suppressing the Jacobites in the North. For these services he was restored

180

PLATE LIV

SIMON FRASER, 12th LORD LOVAT

1667-1747

SIMON LOVAT, 12TH LORD LOVAT.
1667–1747.

to the family estates and title, but some years later he was again in communication with the Old Pretender, and was a party to the invitation of 1740. But when Prince Charles made his great attempt in 1745, Lovat found himself in a tight place. He did not attend the Prince in person, but asked and received a dukedom from him. He assured Lord President Forbes of his loyalty to King George, but requested a warrant to seize Forbes in the Chevalier's name. While apparently supporting the preparations for suppressing the rising, he was actively fomenting it ; and when at last, after Prestonpans, he urged his eldest son, the Master of Lovat, to raise the clan and join the rebels, while he himself would preserve an appearance of neutrality, he had delayed action too long to be of service to Prince Charles, and had become too deeply involved to save himself. Captured in the West Highlands, whither he had fled after Culloden, he was taken to London, tried, found guilty of treason, and executed. He met death with great firmness, joked with the executioner, and, looking at the great crowd assembled at the Tower Hill, wondered why there should be such a bustle about taking off an old grey head from a man who could not get up three steps without assistance.

ALTHOUGH Hogarth is said to have painted Lovat a good while before he made the portrait which connects painter and sitter so closely, the only traceable likeness of earlier date is the mezzotint engraving by John Simon (who died in 1751, but who does not seem to have engraved after 1742), after Le Clare, a bust in armour, the head slightly turned to the left, which shows him in middle life. While it is substantially the same face as that rendered with such remorseless veracity by Hogarth in 1746, the nose is not so flat and short, the eyebrows are less abruptly arched towards the outside of the temples, and the expression is less crafty. It was on August 14 that Hogarth, who went to St. Albans on the invitation of Dr. Webster, Lovat's medical attendant, met the old peer. His lordship was being shaved when Hogarth was introduced, but he rose at once to welcome his visitor, and kissed him on the cheek, a salute which the painter, who got some soap-suds on his face, did not relish greatly. A sitting was arranged for immediately, and the sketch, principally in browns and very slight in execution, now in the National Portrait Gallery, is probably that then painted in the White Hart Inn. The British Museum Print Room, however, has a drawing, in stump and chalk, of the head and shoulders which some consider a preliminary study, and one or two replicas or early copies of the Gallery portrait exist. In 1859 a writer in the *Illustrated London News* stated that the original drawing belonged to Lord Saltoun, but whether this is identical with the Print Room one or not is uncertain. By the 25th of August Hogarth had his well-known etching ready, and it had an enormous sale, the press being kept going night and day to supply the demand. The full title of this print explains the artist's motive: 'Lord Lovat counting the Clans on his fingers,' the action of the hands being exactly that of the sitter when he was telling the painter of the strength of the rebels, 'such a chief had so many men.' It is the source of most other engravings, but in addition many caricatures, such as 'The Beautifull Simone,' 'Lord Lovat a Spinning,' and 'Rebellion Rewarded,' appeared about the time of his trial. According to Carlyle of Inveresk, who met him at Lucky Vint's tavern in 1741, and seems to have been much struck by the flatness of his nose and the thickness of his legs, Lovat was tall and stately, and might have been handsome in his youth; but while Hogarth gives nose and legs of the character indicated, his picture shows a man, of tall stature certainly, but of uncouth and ill-knit figure. A more detailed description of him at the time of his trial, and one which comes very near Hogarth's in vividness, may be found in the *Gentleman's Magazine.* 'Lord Lovat,' it runs, 'makes an odd figure, being generally more loaded with clothes than a Dutchman with his ten pair of breeches; he is tall, walks very upright considering his great age, and is tolerably well shaped; he has a large mouth and short nose, with eyes very much contracted and down-looking, a very small forehead, almost all covered with a large periwig; this gives him a grim aspect, but upon addressing any one he puts on a smiling countenance.'

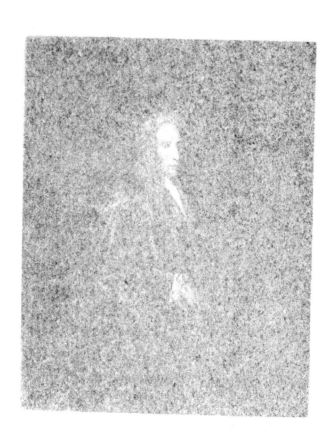

PLATE LV

LORD PRESIDENT
DUNCAN FORBES OF CULLODEN

1685-1747

Painter : JEREMIAH DAVISON (1695-1750?).
Size : 57 × 46 ins.
In the possession of the FACULTY OF ADVOCATES, Parliament House, Edinburgh.

DUNCAN, second son of the Laird of Culloden, was educated at Inverness Grammar School, and, having studied law in Edinburgh and Leyden, was admitted advocate in 1709. The Argyll influence then secured him—for he was an active Whig—the Sheriffship of Midlothian, and during the Rebellion of 1715 his brother and he raised forces in the north to support the Government, and, in combination with Lovat, recaptured Inverness. Being strongly in favour of leniency, he reluctantly accepted the office of Advocate-Depute in the following year, but was not required to prosecute the rebels at Carlisle, and even collected funds for their support. In 1722 Forbes was elected M.P. for the Inverness Burghs, in 1725 he became Lord Advocate, and ten years later he succeeded his brother and set about improving the family estate. Although a Government official, he opposed the bill to penalise Edinburgh for the Porteous mob, but in the same year he was appointed Lord President of the Court of Session, and soon made a great reputation as a judge. His connection with the Highlands gave him special knowledge of their condition, and, amongst other schemes for their amelioration, he suggested raising Highland regiments, an idea afterwards acted upon by Pitt. When Prince Charles landed he succeeded in keeping Macdonald of Sleat and the MacLeod, two of the most powerful chiefs, upon the side of the Government, and his watchfulness hampered Lord Lovat's intrigues and delayed his decision until it was of little account. When the Jacobite hopes were shattered finally on Culloden Moor, Forbes tried to restrain the cruelties of the Duke of Cumberland, who afterwards spoke of him as 'that old woman who talked to me about humanity.' Broken in health and impoverished in fortune by his exertions on behalf of the Government and the best interests of his country, Forbes died on 10th December 1747. In youth he and his brother had been 'the greatest boozers in the north,' but in middle life he moderated these excesses and took a deep interest in religion, concerning which he published (1748) his *Thoughts*. 'I knew and venerated the man,' says Warburton, 'one of the greatest that ever Scotland bred, both as a judge, a patriot, and a Christian.'

FORBES'S best portraits are those painted by J. Davison: a seated three-quarter-length in the Parliament House, and a head and shoulders (34 × 28 ins.) in the possession of the Culloden family, which was at one time attributed to Ramsay. The larger was engraved by Faber in the year following the Lord President's death, and is therefore quite contemporary, while it was used by Roubiliac (1695-1762) as his principal guide when modelling the fine statue in the Parliament Hall. Although over hard and precise in handling, the face is full of character, and the accessories and the general aspect of the canvas are well managed. He has clear blue grey eyes under light eyebrows and a ruddy complexion; and his robes are greenish black with tippet and trimmings of dull purple velvet. The family picture agrees closely with the Advocates' as regards likeness, and is more concentrated in design; and with it, although exaggerating the facial characteristics and greatly inferior in handling, may be grouped the version or copy in the Scottish National Portrait Gallery. The portrait (29⅜ × 24 ins.) in the London Portrait Gallery is also a version of Davison's picture, and not by Aikman as suggested in the official catalogue. Aikman was dead before Forbes was raised to the bench. A water-colour drawing (7 × 4½ ins.) in the Edinburgh Gallery exaggerates the prominent features of Forbes's face to the verge of caricature, but it is signed 'Jos. Campbell, Fecit anno Domini, 1746. Elg., November 20th, 1746,' from which it seems to have been drawn at Elgin only a few months before he died.

AM

PLATE LVI

JAMES THOMSON

1700–1748

Painter: JOHN PATOUN.
Date: 1746.
Size: 29½ × 24 ins.
In the NATIONAL PORTRAIT GALLERY.
Photographic negative by Messrs. Walker and Cockerell.

A SON of the Manse, born at Ednam and brought up at Southdean, the Roxburghshire parishes successively occupied by his father, Thomson was destined and studied for the Church of Scotland until 1725, when, for some reason never fully explained, he went to London suddenly. But whatever the occasion, literary ambition was no doubt the determining factor. Already he had written much poetry, most of which he had, however, destroyed; now, after securing a tutorship in Lord Binning's family, he devoted himself to a poem which was to see print and win its writer fame. 'Winter' was published in 1726, and was followed at intervals by poems on Summer, Spring, and Autumn, until in 1730 *The Seasons* appeared as a complete work. The success achieved by the sections was more than maintained by the whole, and Thomson was hailed as a poet with a new note and a fresh view of things. These are not qualities, indeed, which usually win rapid recognition, and they were probably less obvious to his contemporaries than they are in perspective, but the public was tired of pseudo-pastorals, and, if Thomson's work is not free from that taint, his descriptions of landscape set a new fashion and helped to prepare the way for a return to nature. But, then as now, a poet could make more through a playhouse than a publisher, and in 1730 Thomson's first tragedy, *Sophonisba*, was produced at Drury Lane. He afterwards went abroad for a couple of years with the son of Lord Chancellor Talbot, and on his return was appointed Secretary of Briefs in the Court of Chancery. When Talbot died, the Prince of Wales gave Thomson a pension, and in 1744 his

185

friend, Lord Lyttleton, obtained him a sinecure as Surveyor-General of the Leeward Islands. Meanwhile he had settled in a villa at Richmond, and, though he produced a number of plays (amongst them *The Masque of Alfred*, in which Mallet collaborated, and which is now only remembered for Thomson's 'Rule Britannia'), it was not until the appearance of *The Castle of Indolence*, upon which he was engaged for many years, that he published anything comparable to *The Seasons*, and a few months later he died. Beloved by all his friends, and they included many of the most distinguished of his contemporaries, the tablet erected to his memory bears these words, 'The greatest pain he ever gave his fellow-creatures was that of his death.'

AS Thomson did not arrive in London until 1725, and Aikman, whose acquaintance he had made in Edinburgh a few years before, and who was by then a fashionable painter in the metropolis, died in 1731, his portrait by that artist (which is usually assigned to the earlier year), in the Scottish National Portrait Gallery (oval 21½ × 10½ ins.), represents him as he was while engaged upon, or just after the completion of, the poem which established his fame. It is not, however, one of Aikman's happier efforts: still Pitt thought it 'beastly like,' and it gives a good impression of the poet ere he became the over-fat and lazy person who wrote *The Castle of Indolence*. His face, slightly turned to the right, has rounded cheeks and full red lips, wide clear blue eyes under light brown lashes, and a frank and placid expression: a blue cowl-like cap, below which the hair is confined, sits on his high unwrinkled forehead, he carries his head somewhat jauntily, his shirt is open at the neck, and a fold of a red mantle lies upon the shoulder of his elegant blue velvet coat. The history of this picture is unknown, but it was engraved by J. Basire, who likewise engraved the portrait reproduced for the splendid quarto edition of Thomson's works published in 1762. A second portrait, attributed to Aikman, but in J. M. Gray's opinion more probably by Patoun (a bust [28 × 18 ins.] face three-quarters to the right), is at The Ross, near Hamilton, in the possession of Aikman's relations, who also own a highly interesting terra-cotta bust, signed 'Mich. Rysback, 1738,' which gives the poet a finer type of face than the painted portraits: a curved and more delicately moulded nose, less heavy lips, and a more refined expression: and as replicas appear to be unknown, it may be unique. Here, as in the pictures, he wears a kerchief wound cap fashion on his head, a loose-necked shirt, and an open coat. A portrait (28½ × 28½ ins.),

136

JAMES THOMSON

by an unknown painter, which belongs to the family of Lord Lyttleton, one of the poet's friends, is not unlike Aikman's in type, but has grey eyes. To about the same period as the Edinburgh Aikman, for it shows Thomson in early manhood, one may also assign the interesting picture (21 × 17½ ins.), attributed to William Hogarth, in Mr. Stirling's collection at Keir. Of all the portraits this is the most vivacious: the eyes have a sparkle, the expression an animation, and the poise of the head an alertness only hinted at by Aikman, and completely ignored by Patoun. Hogarth's name is also associated with a second portrait acquired by Sir William Stirling Maxwell and now at Pollok, but it is of less moment. Between the more youthful portraits and the last, in 1736, Stephen Slaughter, an Irish artist who was Keeper of the King's pictures and died in 1765, painted the Dryburgh Abbey likeness, of which Lord Buchan (for whose Thomson festival in 1791 Burns wrote his verses to the poet of *The Seasons*) presented a miniature copy, still preserved in the manse, to the long defunct Ednam Club. The Patoun, which was presented to the London Gallery in 1857 by Thomson's grand-niece, Miss Bell of Spring Hall, Coldstream, was painted two years before Thomson died. His fat, fair-complexioned, double-chinned face has bright yellow brown eyes and broad, dark brown eyebrows, indolence is written on his countenance, and the blue nightcap and dressing-gown he wears suggest the slippered ease and negligence of his last years. 'Thomson,' says Dr. Johnson, 'was of a stature above middle size, and "more fat than bard beseems," of a dull countenance, and a gross, unanimated, uninteresting appearance, silent in mingled company, but cheerful among select friends, and by his friends very tenderly and warmly beloved.'

PLATE LVII
ALEXANDER ROBERTSON
OF STRUAN

'THE POET CHIEF'

1670 ?–1749

Painter and date : unknown.
Size : oval 28 × 21 ins.
In the Scottish National Portrait Gallery.

WHILE being educated at St. Andrews University, with a view to entering the Church, the death of his father and half-brother made him chief of his clan (1688), and Viscount Dundee having raised the Highlands for King James, Robertson turned out with his men. Although still a minor and not present at Killiecrankie, not having joined the rebels until the day after, he was attainted for his share in the rising, and taking refuge with the exiled King at St. Germains, served in the French army until he received a remission and returned to Rannoch. In 1715, however, he took five hundred clansmen to fight under Mar for the Chevalier. Struan was taken prisoner and rescued at Sheriffmuir, and being recaptured escaped a second time, and after many adventures reached France. Pardoned again (1731), he was too old to follow Prince Charles in person, but he was present at Prestonpans, and seven hundred of his clan were out in the '45. Still he had taken no part in the actual fighting, and in consideration of his age the old Jacobite escaped prescription, and died at home.

His poems, which were collected and published shortly after his death, have been frequently reissued. They owe their interest to association more than to merit, but that has been sufficient to earn him his distinctive appellation.

LVII

ROBERTSON

STRUAN

ALEXANDER ROBERTSON OF STRUAN
(1670?-1749)

ALEXANDER ROBERTSON OF STRUAN

THE only known portrait of 'the poet chief' is that bequeathed to the Edinburgh Portrait Gallery by Mr. Robertson of Struan. As becomes one who had been out thrice in the Stuart cause, he is represented in the act of drinking the health of the King 'over the water,' his raised left hand holding a glass of red wine above the water-bottle held in his right. He has grey eyebrows and very dark eyes, and wears a dark brown wig. There are traces of an inscription on the background, but 'Uiue le R' (Vive le Roi) is all that is legible.

PLATE LVIII

SIR JOHN CLERK, BART.

BARON OF EXCHEQUER

1676–1755

Painter: WILLIAM AIKMAN (1682-1731).
Size: 50 × 40 ins.
In the possession of Sir GEORGE DOUGLAS CLERK, Bart., of Penicuik.

IF Sir John Clerk has no claim to rank as one of the greatest Scotsmen of the eighteenth century, his was an interesting personality, and he left an autobiography (edited by the late J. M. Gray for the Scottish History Society) and an account of his travels which not only reveal him as a man of strong and fine character, but throw valuable side-lights on the life of his time. He was born in 1676—not in 1684 as has usually been stated—and, after studying for a while at Glasgow College, went to the great school of law at Leyden, where he became the intimate friend of Herman Boerhaave, then at the beginning of the career which was to make him the most famous physician in Europe. Leaving Leyden after three years' residence, he travelled in Germany, Italy, France, and Flanders, and, returning home, passed advocate. He had learned much besides law, and after referring to that he sums up :—

' My improvements abroad were these. I spoke French and Italian very well, but particularly Dutch, having come very young to Holland, and kept more in the company of Hollanders than those of my own country.

' I had applied much to classical learning, and had more than ordinary inclination for Greek and Roman antiquities.

' I understood pictures better than became my purse, and as to musick I performed better, specially on the herpiscord, than became a gentleman.'

In 1702 he entered Parliament and sat for Whithorn until the Union; and, having acted as Commissioner, he was appointed one of the Barons of the new Court of Exchequer. Thereafter his life was uneventful but full: he had his

PLATE LVIII

SIR JOHN CLERK, BART.

BARON OF EXCHEQUE

1684

...which was... ...age of ...years... ...fashion of...
...persuaded... ...the bill an...
...by... ...the J. M. Gray for the Scottish History
...which... ...as a man of
...of... ...now and... ...lights on the ink of his time.
...born... ...1684 as has already been noted... after
...Glas... ...was Crown... went to... ...part... ...of law at
...who... ...at the house... ...of Herman Boerhaave, then at the
...for which was to make him the most accomplished in
...Lawyer... ...three years and... ...travelled in Germany,
...Flanders... ...and... ...having been pressed into...years... He had
...has... ...and not returning to the... ...be some...
...tastes... ...I spoke French and Italian very
...ly Dutch, having become very young too... and kept
...of Holland... ...than those of my own country
...much to classical learning, and had more than ordinary
...Greek and Roman antiquities.
...was better than been... ...my purse, and as to manners I
...Scot... ...by on the Continent than to a mere gentleman'
...Parliament... ...as for Whithorn... the Union; and
...Commissioner, he was appointed one... the Barons of the new
...Court... ...lot... ...he was so... that but that he had his
...

THE ... OF THE ... MASTER OF THE ROLLS
17.. — 17..

PLATE LVIII

SIR JOHN CLERK, BART.

BOX OF EXCHEQUER

the lives of these great men of ... being prosecuted and he left an ... the Rev. J. M. Gray for the Scottish History ... when not over pressed was a man of ... which satisfied his method of his times.

Just as has usually been celebrated, after ... Orleans went to the universal of law at ... friend of Herman Boerhaave then at the ... made him the most famous physician in ... years ... he travelled in Germany, ... of a journey and afterwards. He had ... a disposing of the class in apprecia... conversant with men ... I speak French and Italian very ... and being come a very young ... scholar, and kept ... Holidays than those of my own country ...

... much to classical learning, and I set more than enough ... and Roman antiquities ...

... at pictures better than I could ... my purse, and as to medals I ... severely on the days and then become a gentleman ...

... Parliament and set the Whigs turned the Tories and ... he was created one of the Barons of the new ... I was too often bit this he had his

SIR JOHN CLERK, BART.

official duties and his estates to attend to, his studies and his friendships with authors and artists to cultivate, and now and then he wrote a learned pamphlet or turned the stave of a song.

FOUR portraits of the Baron are owned by his family. The earliest is a pencil drawing made at Leyden, when he was 'ætatis 19,' by (Willem?) van Mieris, with whom he tells us he studied drawing. The others show him in later life. Two are by Sir John Medina, but the third, by the Baron's own cousin, William Aikman, is far finer than either. In it he wears his official black robe over a yellow brown coat, and the figure is simply posed against an almost plain background. It is an excellent example of Aikman's refined and serious style at its very best.

PLATE LIX

JAMES FRANCIS EDWARD KEITH

MARSHAL KEITH

1696-1758

Painter: FRANCESCO TREVISANI (1656-1746).
Size: 47 × 36 ins.
In the possession of the EARL OF KINTORE.

BORN at Inverugie Castle, the second son of the ninth Earl Marischal, he was educated under Bishop Keith and at Marischal College, Aberdeen; but the Rebellion of 1715, when he and his brother the Earl were out, gave him his first taste of the soldiering for which he had sighed. In exile, however, he resumed his studies at Paris, and became a member of the Académie des Sciences. But, after the ill-starred Jacobite attempt in Scotland in 1719, he adopted the profession of arms definitely, and, having served for some years in the Spanish army, he, in 1728, entered that of Russia. His promotion was rapid, for he served in many campaigns with the greatest distinction, and was highly esteemed by the Empress Anna, who declared that she would sooner loose ten thousand of her best soldiers than Keith. With her successor, Elizabeth, he also stood well, but intrigues against him as a foreigner at last compelled him to leave Russia, and Frederick the Great at once secured his services and created him a field-marshal. His career in Frederick's army, the many famous battles and sieges in which he took part until the fatal field at Hochkirck, on which he fell, may not be recounted here, but by universal consent Marshal Keith is the greatest soldier of the many Scots who have served with distinction in foreign armies. His grateful master erected a statue to him in Berlin, and he is a prominent figure amongst those grouped round the pedestal of Frederick's own famous statue in the Unter den Linden.

PLATE LIX

FRANCIS EDWARD KEITH

MARSHAL KEITH

FIELD-MARSHALL JAMES KEITH
1696 - 1758
PAINTED BY FRANCIS C. GOODMAN

JAMES FRANCIS EDWARD KEITH

A THREE-QUARTER-LENGTH by Alexis Simon Belle (1674-1734) in Marischal College, Aberdeen, is perhaps the earliest portrait of Marshal Keith. It represents him as a man of about thirty, with refined features, clearly marked eyebrows, straight nose, drooping slightly at the point, and a mouth which, in combination with his frank expression, suggests a genial and kindly nature. He wears dark armour, the figure is three-quarters turned to the left, his left hand rests on a scarlet scarf about his waist, and his right, in which he holds a baton, is laid upon a helmet in the left lower corner. As Keith went to Russia in 1728, this picture, of which an excellent reproduction appears in Mr. P. J. Anderson's *Fasti. Acad. Marisc.*, vol. ii., was probably painted about that time. That by Allan Ramsay (1713-1784), engraved in mezzotint by A. Van Haecken, shows him some ten or twelve years later, when he visited this country (February to May 1740) with his brother. There seems no record of his having visited Edinburgh, but, as Ramsay had not yet gone to London, he may have done so, and the plate was certainly executed before 1747, for it describes him as 'General-in-Chief of the Armies of His Imperial Majesty of all ye Russias,' and Keith entered Frederick's service in the year mentioned. A bust in armour, with a fur-lined cloak over the right shoulder and the left arm cut off by the frame at the elbow, he faces straight out, and the nose appears less aquiline, and the chin is heavier and deeper than in the earlier picture and in that reproduced, which, if the ascription to Trevisani (1656-1746) is used as a limit, must have been painted before Keith was fifty, and certainly several years later than the Ramsay. The likeness between this and the early portrait by Belle, in both features and expression, is notable, and in both he bears considerable resemblance to his brother, the Earl, which he does not in Ramsay's picture or in that engraved in 1758 by A. Baillie, from an original in Lord Galloway's possession. Painted by Antoine Pesne (1684-1757), Frederick the Great's court painter and Director of the Academy in Berlin, the expression of face in the last is nearer the Ramsay than the others described, but it exaggerates the geniality to the verge of caricature, and is exceedingly theatrical in pose and arrangement.

PLATE LX

ALLAN RAMSAY

1686-1758

Painter : WILLIAM AIKMAN (1682-1731).
Date : 1723.
Size : 30 × 25 ins.
In the possession of Sir GEORGE DOUGLAS CLERK, Bart., of Penicuik.

WIG-MAKER and bookseller, poet and would-be theatrical impresario, Allan Ramsay was born in the highest village of southern Scotland, where his father managed Lord Hopetoun's lead-mines. Going to Edinburgh, he learned the art of trimming wigs, and tried his hand at writing verses, in which he hit off the humours of the time and delineated with rare gusto the life about him in the old grey city of steep streets and narrow wynds and closes and many-storied lands. By 1721 his poems and songs, many of which had appeared as broadsides and been hawked about the town, were numerous enough to make a quarto volume, and in 1725 he dedicated *The Gentle Shepherd*, the pastoral in virtue of which he occupies a distinctive place amongst poets, to the charming Countess of Eglinton. But ere this he had abandoned wig-making for bookselling, and had set up the first circulating library in Scotland, while some ten years later he built a theatre—in Carrubber's Close—only to scandalise the community and have it closed by the city fathers. He also edited—over-edited, literary purists say—*The Tea-Table Miscellany* and *The Evergreen*, two collections of Scottish poetry in which many old pieces were partially preserved, and some modern, such as Lady Wardlaw's fine ballad, 'Hardyknute,' passed for such. His own poetry revived the flagging springs of Scottish song, and he was the precursor of Fergusson and Burns.

THE frontispiece to the first quarto edition of the poet's works, published by Ruddiman in 1721, is probably his earliest portrait, but the location of the original is unknown. Engraved by T. Vercruysse, it bears initials 'J. S. P.,'

144

PLATE LX

ALLAN RAMSAY

ALLAN RAMSAY, bookseller, poet, and would-be ....d .. presents .... Poet .. ... born in the highest village of .. w ... Scotland. .... a manager of Lord Hopetoun's ... ... Going to ... ... he ... ... of a trimming wig, and tried ... ... at writing verses, in which ... . the humours of the time and remained ... ... gossip of ... ... the old grey city of steep streets and ... ... is ... ... By 1721 his poems and ... ... many of which had ... ... as broadsides and been hawked about ... town, were ... ... into a quarto volume, and in 17... he dedicated *The* ... ... the portrait in virtue of which he is ... ... native place ... ... the interesting Chambers of Edinburgh ... ... but even this he had ... ... starting for bookselling, and had set up the first circulating library ... ... some ... ... later he built a ... ... in Ramsay's Close ... ... the community an have it closed by the electric ... ... He also ... ... literary publications — *The Tea-Table* ... ... and *The* ... ... collections of Scottish poetry in which many old pieces were ... ... some modern, such as Lucy Wardlaw's fine ballad, ... his side. His own poetry revived the bubbling springs ... ... was the precursor of Fergusson and Burns.

THE ... ... the first quarto edition of the poet's works, published ... ... Edinburgh in 17... is probably his earliest portrait, but the location ... ... is ... ... are mean. Engraved by T. Vercruy ... it bears initials A. S. P.

412

which stand for 'John Smibert, Pinxit,' an intimate friend of Allan, who is also credited with the portrait at New Hall, Midlothian, which belonged to the poet's daughter and is supposed to be the source of the engraving by A. Wilson, which embellishes an edition of *The Gentle Shepherd* (Edinburgh, 1814). Seven years later Ruddiman issued another edition, in the second volume of which a print, inscribed, 'R. Cooper, ad vivum sculpsit, Eden^n,' appeared; but stolid and heavy in expression, and poorly drawn, it is of little value. In the following year, however, the poet's artist son, then just sixteen years old, made a sketch in black chalk ($15\frac{3}{4} \times 12$ ins.)—'His first attempt of that kind from the life, 1729,' as it is marked—which, despite indecision of drawing, is highly characteristic and interesting. It belongs to the Fraser-Tytlers of Woodhouselee. To the younger Allan we are also indebted for the vigorous profile which was engraved, 'A. Ramsay, ad. viv. del. D. Allan, Sc. Edin.,' as frontispiece for the edition of *The Gentle Shepherd* issued by the celebrated Foulis press in 1788 and illustrated by David Allan with those aquatints after his own drawings, in which, with other of that artist's work, the Scottish genre picture may be said to have originated. With a fairly high forehead swelling prominently at the eyebrows, a clear-cut but slightly up-turned nose, full lips, of which the under is rather heavy, and a small peaked chin, with a slight double between point and throat, this rendering is pretty convincing; and the mask and the shepherd's staff and horn to left and right of the panel beneath, which bears 'Allan Ramsay, Scotus' in bold letters, add a symbolical touch. The black chalk drawing touched with white on blue grey paper (oval $6\frac{3}{4} \times 5\frac{3}{4}$ ins.), which was assigned to Richardson (1665-1745) when in Cunningham's possession, but was attributed to Aikman (1682-1731) by W. Bell Scott, H.R.S.A (1811-1890), who presented it to the Scottish National Portrait Gallery, is much more likely to be by his son. It is signed 'Allan Ramsay,' and dated 'Feb. 1745,' at which time Richardson had long retired from the practice of his art and Aikman had been dead nearly fifteen years, and is quite in the younger Ramsay's style. But in spirit, vivacity, and convincing quality, none of these rivals the portrait reproduced. Painted in 1728, as is certified by Baron Clerk, who wrote on the back of the canvas,

A ROUNDLET IN MR. RAMSAY'S OWN WAY.

Here painted on this canvass clout,
By Aikman's hand, is Ramsay's snout;
The picture's value none might doubt,
For ten to one I 'll venture,

SCOTTISH PORTRAITS

The great criticks could not tell
Which of the two does most excell,
Or in his way should bear the bell,
    The Poet or the Painter.

J. C., Pennicuik, 5 May 1753.

It represents the poet in his prime, two years before *The Gentle Shepherd* was given to the world, and, as Burns would have said, when it was on the wheels. Here he wears a brown coat over a shirt open at the neck, and his pert pawky face, with its *retroussé* nose, dark eyes and bushy eyebrows, is relieved against a simple background upon which the orange kerchief, wound tightly round his head, and looking like the nightcap one has come to associate with the little poet, strikes a rich full note.

$\frac{1}{598}$ L. $\frac{n}{2}$

Lightning Source UK Ltd.
Milton Keynes UK
UKOW02f0008110214

226247UK00007B/704/P